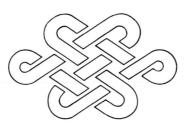

CHINESE
KNOTTING

CHINESE KNOTTING

Creative designs that are easy and fun!

by Lydia Chen

TUTTLE PUBLISHING
Boston • Rutland, Vermont • Tokyo

Published in 2003 by Tuttle Publishing,
an imprint of Periplus Editions by
arrangement with Echo Publishing Co. Ltd.

ISBN 0-8048-3399-0

Distributed by:

North America, Latin America & Europe
Tuttle Publishing
Airport Industrial Park, 364 Innovation
Drive, North Clarendon, VT 05759-9436
Tel: (802) 773 8930 Fax: (802) 7736993
Email: info@tuttlepublishing.com

Japan
Tuttle Publishing
Yaekari Building, 3rd Floor, 5-4-12 Osaki,
Shinagawa-ku, Tokyo 141-0032
Tel: (03) 5437 0171 Fax: (03) 5437 0755
Email: tuttle-sales@gol.com

Asia Pacific
Berkeley Books Pte. Ltd.
130 Joo Seng Road, #06-01/03 Singapore
368357
Tel: (65) 62801330 Fax: (65) 6280 6290
Email: inquiries@periplus.com.sg

09 08 07 06 05 04
7 6 5 4

Printed in Singapore

CREDITS: Cover, Huang Yung-sung; pages
13-15, courtesy of Lydia Chen; 16, 17, 19, 20,
22, 24, 30, 31-39, Huang Yung-sung; 18, Yao
Meng-chia; 21, 95, 100, 102, 105, 108, 110,
112, Chuang Ling and Huang Yung-sung; 23,
89, 91, 97, Chuang Ling; 42-58, 60-87, 90-
115, illustrations by Li Sheng-ta, Li Li-wen, Lai
Chun-sheng, and Kuo Chuan-chu.

This book is dedicated
to the countless Chinese women who
left us the knotting legacy and
people all over the world
working to keep their folk arts
alive and growing.

PUBLISHER'S FOREWORD

This book introduces readers and crafts people to the fascinating world of Chinese knotting. Sometimes referred to as Chinese macramé, Chinese knotting is a craft increasingly gaining popularity in both the East and the West as more and more people come to realize the benefits of traditional handwork in a world of urban industrialization, mass production, modern transportation, and computer technology. This traditional craft provides not only a wonderful means of relaxation but also allows the artistic satisfaction of producing a personalized work of art.

Chinese knotting, literally "the joining of two cords", is an ancient and revered art form in China and an integral part of Chinese life. Since ancient times, Chinese knots have been fashioned from cotton and silk for a variety of practical and decorative purposes: to record events, aid in fishing and hunting, wrap and tie items, embellish personal attire, ornament other works of art, and communicate. The earliest recorded use of decorative knots is on bronze vessels dating to the Warring States Period (700 BC). Chinese knots have decorated both the fixtures of palace halls and the daily implements of country folk. They have also appeared in paintings, sculptures, and folk art. In Chinese poetry, knots symbolize the emotional ties of lovers, and ornamental knots are traditional keepsakes exchanged by lovers.

In China, up until the late 1930s, decorative knotting was a widespread pastime. On festive occasions and during important rites of passage such as weddings, intricate and beautiful knots, tied by family and friends, could be seen everywhere, lending both a festive and personal air to important occasions. The knots were an aesthetic expression of Chinese folk symbolism, expressing wishes for good fortune and wealth or the joys of love and marriage.

From the 1930s up until the late 1970s, when the art of macramé became popular in the West – causing a simultaneous revival of interest in Chinese knotting – traditional knotting was barely seen except in museums where examples were shown as relics of an ancient culture or in antique shops where they were greedily snapped up by foreign buyers intrigued by the intricate craftsmanship and the magnificent color combinations of the exquisitely symmetrical knots on sale.

In this book, the author, Lydia Chen, a well-known and highly respected authority on Chinese knotting and a pioneer in the revival of Chinese knotting, first traces the evolution of the craft, piecing together scraps of evidence that have trickled down through research into historical texts, the examination of both archaeological finds and items in public and private collections, and interviews with aged Chinese folk artists.

This knowledge has been assembled in a practical manual that takes readers through the fundamental elements necessary for tying Chinese decorative knots: the materials and implements required, and the processes of tying, tightening, and adding the finishing touches to knots. There are step-by-step instructions for the eleven basic knots, which are named

according to their distinctive shapes, use, or origins. The double coin knot, for example, shaped like two overlapping coins of the type once used in ancient China, is regarded as a symbol of prosperity and was once hung by merchants over their shops to attract wealth. The pan chang or mystic knot, one of the eight Buddhist treasures, twists and turns in a seemingly endless pattern, a graphic representation of the cyclical nature of life.

The basic knots provide the building blocks for the 14 compound knots – combinations and variations of the simple knots – that follow. In them, the basic knots are brought together to form more complex and significant configurations drawn from nature, folk imagination, and the Chinese language. The longevity knot, the double happiness knot, the dragon knot, and the crane knot are examples. Rich in imagery and aesthetically pleasing to the eye, they make fine decorative items by themselves.

The last part of the book presents diagrams and textual explanations for 41 knotted creations of varying difficulty that readers can put to use in everyday life: necklaces with and without knotted pendants, knotted belts and wrap-around sashes, buttons, purse fasteners, and wall and plant hangings. Once the knots in this book have been mastered, the sky is the limit for the creative and dedicated knotter. The endless variations and the elegant patterns that can be generated, combined with the multitude of materials that can be used (silk, cotton, nylon, leather, straw, precious and semiprecious stones, etc.) have expanded the applications and functions of Chinese knotting.

Once an oral tradition, handed down from generation to generation, Chinese knotting is now accessible to anyone interested in hand craft and in Chinese culture. The technical section of Chinese Knotting, along with the historical and symbolic background of the knots themselves, will allow readers to participate in a Chinese cultural tradition as they learn about it. Detailed step-by-step instructions, clear diagrams, and color photographs of both the knots and their applications in everyday use will aid both beginning and more experienced knotters and provide endless hours of pleasure.

AUTHOR'S FOREWORD

When I was young, writing a book on traditional Chinese decorative knotting was as inconceivable to me as time travel is now. I was too busy climbing trees and playing ball to sit still long enough to tie my shoelaces, let alone a decorative knot.

Even while I was in college, sports continued to occupy most of my thoughts, with perhaps some time spared for my major in agricultural chemistry. No matter how you look at it, both my curricular and extracurricular activities were just about as far afield from folk arts as I could get.

An unexpected twist of events, however, changed the course of my life. It started about ten years ago when Wang Chen-kai, a master knotter from Mainland China, began working at the National Palace Museum in Taipei. My late father-in-law, Chuang Shang-yen, who was Deputy Curator at the Museum, urged me to learn whatever I could from Wang. I did not think that anything would come from it. Still, I had a bit of free time and I thought the knots were attractive, so I began tying my first knots.

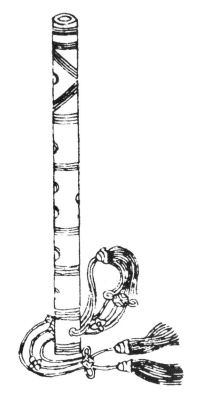

Soon I was trying my hand at tying more and more difficult knots, and I found my interest growing. I was thrilled when I learned that ECHO Magazine was doing a series of articles on Chinese knotting in 1976. I bought the issues and practiced tying the 13 simple knots taught in the magazine until I could tie each and every one of them with my eyes closed. From that point on, I was determined to learn everything I could about this ancient art.

In 1978, I received a surprise call from Chang Ching-shih, the dean of Shih Chien College of Home Economics. He had decided to start a course in Chinese knotting, and wanted me to teach the class. Although I was just a novice knotter then, Dean Chang had no one else to turn to. He flattered, chided, and cajoled me, and somehow, against my better instincts, I agreed to take on the task.

Luckily for me there were still three months to go before the fall semester began. I spent that time practicing my knots day and night. I tracked down antiques with knots I had never seen before, and then spent hours trying to figure out how each of them had been tied. I created a few knots of my own, and experimented with a wide variety of cords. Then in September, with knots in my stomach as well as in my hands, I walked into my first class.

Knotting was an idea whose time had come again. The next fall my teaching load at Shih Chien tripled, and people from all walks of life — jewelers, clothiers, students, housewives, even businessmen — were asking me for private lessons.

It was heartwarming to see such fresh interest in this old folk art tradition. But not everyone has the time or the inclination to enroll in a home economics college, nor could I take on the entire populace

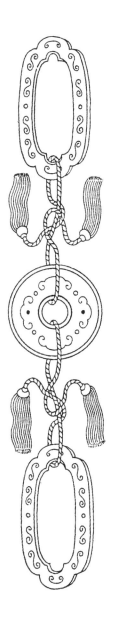

as private students. And except for the ECHO Magazine articles, there was no literature on the subject. I thought the time had come to put out a comprehensive instruction manual on the art of Chinese decorative knotting.

Of course, I had neither the experience nor the wherewithal to publish a book on my own. I knew how to tie the knots and how to teach others to tie them, but I knew little about writing, editing, photography, layout, or financing the publication of such a book. ECHO came to my aid again. They said that if I would put together the material, they would handle all the editorial and technical work involved in publishing an English as well as a Chinese edition. By doing so, they have not only earned my gratitude, but the gratitude of everyone who wants to learn Chinese knotting or see the tradition regain its hold on life.

I hope that you will find our effort both informative and practical. If even a handful of people can use this book to find some of the pleasure that knotting has given me, I will be more than satisfied. As I would express it in Chinese, I will feel I have given a brick in exchange for a piece of fine jade.

January, 1981 Lydia Chen

CONTENTS

INTRODUCTION

The *Shuo Wen Chieh Tzu*, a Chinese dictionary compiled around 100 A.D., defines the word "knot" as "the joining of two cords." Archaeological research indicates that such coupling, originally a necessary sewing skill, may have been going on for tens of thousands of years in China. But over the centuries, knots began to take on functions in and of themselves, and were eventually appreciated for their intricate beauty as well. The art form of traditional decorative knotting was thus born.

Unfortunately the silk cords used to tie traditional knots were highly prone to decay. The only complete specimens of traditional Chinese knotting surviving today are works from the late Ching Dynasty and the early Republican period. Despite the age of these pieces, their intricate knotwork and magnificent color combinations are still enough to take one's breath away.

In those days, decorative knots were tied to wind chimes, palace lanterns, eyeglass cases, fan tassels, hair pins, and a multitude of other objects. They were in effect decorations of decorations, lending elegance and a subtle flavor to objects that would otherwise seem commonplace. The Chinese pursued this ornamentation as a serious art form, and devoted prodigious amounts of time and energy to the perfection of new and more intricate knots. What remains of their work is not only a marvel of technical ingenuity — it is the result of a people's creative spirit searching for aesthetic expression.

To study the design of Chinese knots is to enter the world of Chinese folk symbols of good fortune. In the pages ahead, you will encounter designs fashioned after symbols of longevity, happiness, Buddhist treasures, prosperity, and the commonality of all being, to name just a few.

On a more personal level, it is impossible to look at one of the old knots without wondering about the life of the knotter. How many hopes and dreams worked their way into the interlaced loops and twists as the single strand of cord wound its way into a complete, perfect figure? The knots are almost a study of life itself.

Paleolithic needles showing knotting existed 100,000 years ago in China.

Chou Dynasty bodkins used to untie knots.

4th century painting showing women wearing knotted waist sashes.

2nd century B.C. jug decorated with a knotted motif.

In China, knotting was not only a fine art, but also a form of communication whereby people could express blessings, best wishes, and amorous sentiments.

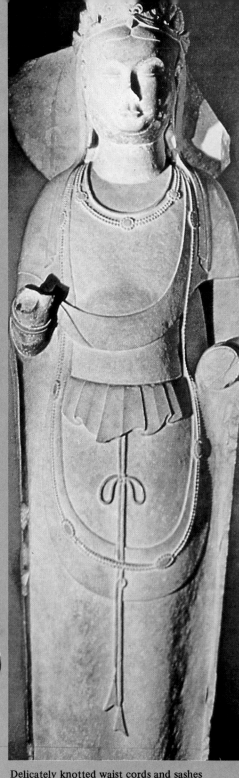

Delicately knotted waist cords and sashes
adorn these Tang Dynasty statues.

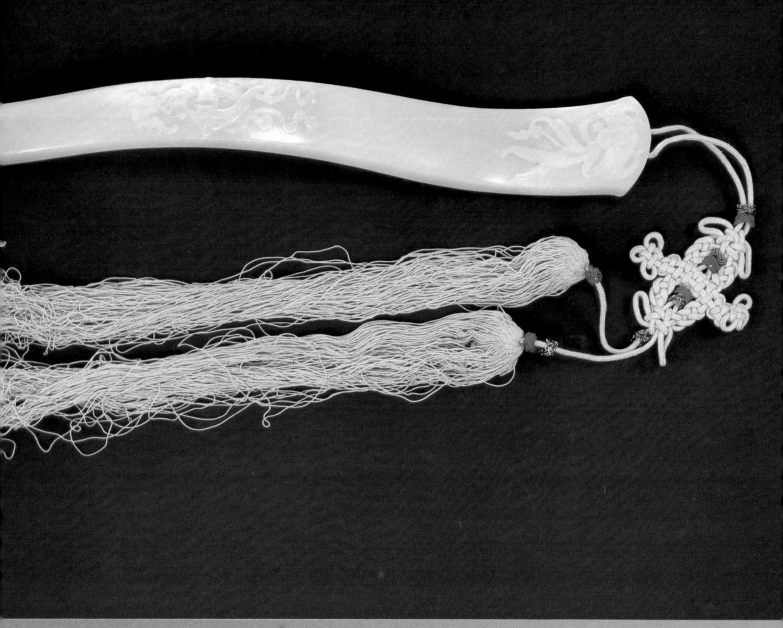

From the bone needles of a hundred thousand years ago to the paintings and statues from imperial China showing traditional flowing robes held shut with knotted sashes, it is clear that knots have long been an integral part of Chinese daily life. Unfortunately, the only complete knotting specimens that survive intact are less than a century old, from an era when knots were used to ornament other works of art — their beauty often unnoticed as they were merely meant to enhance the objects they adorned.

Clockwise from above: decorative knots adorning a woman's sachet; knotting attached to a bed canopy; a grand ensemble from a Ching woman's trousseau; and an eyeglass case with ornamental knotting from the Ching Dynasty.

During the late Ching Dynasty and the early Republican period, exquisite knots made of the finest silk cords graced tobacco pouches, eyeglass cases, sachets, and a host of other everyday items, adding a touch of gaiety and enchantment to a way of life which emphasized propriety and sobriety.

In 1976, ECHO Magazine searched out the few remaining keepers of the knotting tradition in Taiwan. Pictured here is Mrs. Chen Pao, who at the age of 76 reached far back into her memory and used her weathered, trembling hands to teach us her craft. Unfortunately, shortly after ECHO's visit, she fell ill and passed away. Her death underlines how close decorative knotting was to extinction, and how important it is to record and revitalize this and other folk arts before they fade into oblivion.

The human hand is a miraculous organ, and one would be hard pressed to find better proof of this than in the craftsmanship and ingenuity of Chinese decorative knotting. With nothing more than a simple piece of cord and two sensitive hands, generations of Chinese women have created unsung masterpieces of aesthetic expression.

Handmade decorations create a special aura of individuality however they are used. Chinese knots can lend a bit of Oriental delicacy to flutes, paintings, lamps, fans, seals, even the latest fashions — subtly enhancing the appeal of anything they grace.

Chinese knots are much more than mere eye-catchers; many are ripe with symbolic connotations. Borrowing from a rich trove of traditional decorative motifs, the knots can express wishes for good fortune and wealth, the joys of matrimony, and even the loftiest of religious ideals.

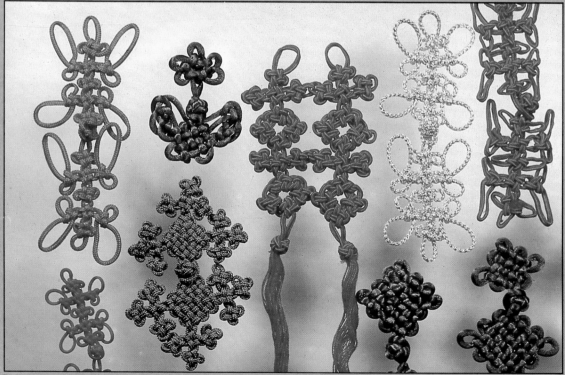

Decorative and imaginative clothes fasteners.

ORIGIN & HISTORY

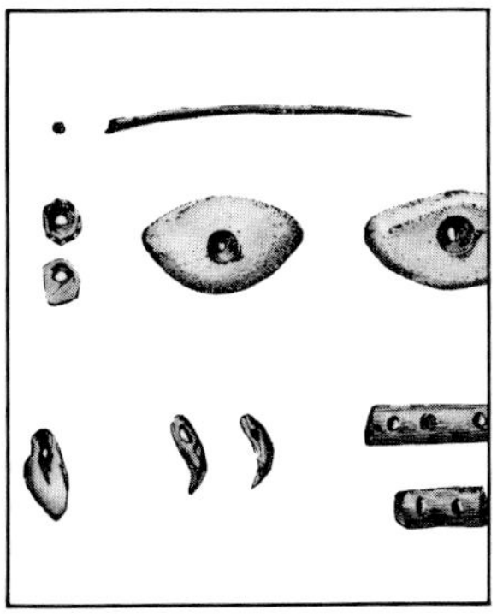

100,000-year-old bone needles and pierced objects unearthed at Choukoutien.

The evolution of Chinese knotting has followed a long and elusive trail that leads back to the silence of remotest antiquity. Chinese culture and the numerous folk arts that thrive in this milieu reach to the dawn of recorded history and beyond. Here, in the valley of the Yellow River, was a cradle of civilization that gave birth to beliefs, customs, and traditions that survive to this day. Folk art, including decorative knotting, is no exception.

Unfortunately, Chinese knotting, ancient as it may be, was never the subject of scholarly treatises. Instead, it remained in the background, a marginal art that was often overlooked. All we have in our hands today are fine examples of knotting from the late Ching and early Republican periods, creations of our grandparents and their parents. The complexity of these knots and the ingenuity of their designs bespeak the culmination of a long, unbroken artistic tradition. Secondhand traces of this ancient folk tradition appear here and there, and the inferences drawn from these tantalizing bits of evidence suggest that the origin of Chinese knotting predates even the possibility of written record.

The first hint of the earliest Chinese knots dates back to the late paleolithic age, seventy to a hundred thousand years ago. Artifacts found from that era in a cave at Choukoutien include several awl-shaped instruments with holes in one end. Archaeologists maintain that they were used for sewing, implying that thread and some rudimentary form of knotting must have existed at that time.

Tenuous as this remote and humble beginning may be, there is no doubt that later inhabitants of the Yellow River basin had need of highly developed knotting techniques. In a commentary on the trigrams of the *Book of Changes*, we discover that "in prehistoric times, events were recorded by tying knots; in later ages, books were used for this." In the second century A.D., the Han scholar Cheng Hsuan expanded on this passage to say that great events were recorded with large knots, and smaller knots signified events of lesser importance. Of course, no samples from prehistory exist.

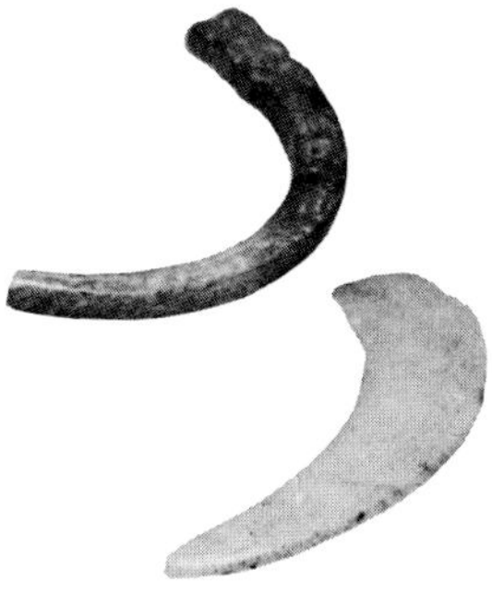

Bodkins used by men of the Chou Dynasty to untie knots.

The only indigenous evidence of this practice consists of simple pictorial representations of the symbolic use of knotting in the Warring States Period, from the fourth to the second century B.C. Number symbols on the surface of bronzeware from that age clearly reflect the earlier practice of making records with knotted cord. For example, the numbers 10, 20, 30, and 40 — 十, 廿, 卅, 卌 — were tied ϯ, U, Ш, and ШU. The similarity between the rope figures and the script forms is striking. On the other hand, these knots represent rather simple abstract concepts. The design of the necessarily more complex and intricate knots that were tied to record events during Chinese prehistory must be left to the imagination. But turning to a satellite

Detail from Ku Kai-chih's "Admonitions of the Court Instructress" showing a knotted sash.

A bronze vessel from the Warring States era, decorated with a knotted motif.

culture, the Ryukyu Islands off China's southeastern coast, we can find concrete examples of intricately knotted ropes that are used to keep records. Perhaps these reflect the ancient Chinese knots that were used in a similar way. The examples from the Ryukyu Islands and the numbers on ancient Chinese bronzes tend to lend credence to the assertion that at least a part of the Chinese written language evolved from these knotted cords. At the very least, they establish the fact that knotting was an abstracted form of symbolic communication that predates the *Book of Changes.*

Other evidence leads to the conclusion that knots were cherished not only as symbols, but also as an essential part of everyday life. Chinese gentlemen of the Chou Dynasty, 1112-256 B.C., carried a special tool tied to their waist sashes, a *hsi.* Made of ivory, jade, and bone, *hsi* have been preserved in a number of museum collections. Their cresent-like shape with one tapered end suggest that they could have been used to loosen knots. Indeed, the *Shuo Wen,* one of the earliest Chinese dictionaries, tells us that the *hsi* was "a device to untie knots, part of adult attire." Knots that called for a special tool to untie them must have been intricate, indeed. Moreover, the fact that a *hsi* was common to all adult wardrobes tells us that knots abounded in the Chou Dynasty, as commonplace as watches are today.

For example, the same gentlemen who could not leave home without their *hsi* were also fond of wearing elaborate belt ornaments hung from their waist sashes. These ornaments were composed of several small pieces of jade — delicately carved dragons, circlets, squares with holes in the centers, crescents, and the like — all strung together in a symmetrical array. Although jade belt ornaments with cord eyelets have been found dating from the Shang and Chou Dynasties, the cords that held them together have long since turned to dust. But surely such prized ornaments warranted equally attractive cord mounting, calling for intricate knotwork between each piece of carved jade.

Long robes with flowing sleeves, the traditional garb of both men and women, had to be fastened at the waist with knotted sashes. Simple examples exist in paintings, but it is not hard to imagine the Chinese of days long gone taking great care in tying their sashes, much as 17th century Europeans were fond of tying elaborate cravats. Looking elsewhere for a hint of these knots, perhaps the intricately knotted Japanese *obi* is not too far removed from earlier Chinese knotted attire.

Household objects in ancient China also made use of knots. Bronze mirrors were forged with rings on their backsides, so that they could be tied to walls by knotted cords. Although the earthenware jugs of old have long since disappeared, ceremonial bronze replicas of them from the Warring States Period retain a design of the knotted network that was used to hoist them. The fact that the knotted pattern was retained in the bronze replicas is interesting in and of itself, because it represents the first surviving use of a knotting motif for a purely decorative purpose.

With knots playing such an important role in personal apparel and household items, and having already been used symbolically, it was quite natural for the ever-artistic Chinese to further explore the decora-

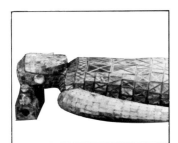

Jade plate-mail burial suit of Han Princess Tou Wan.

String of knots decorating the back of a sash on a Tang tri-color figurine.

tive possibilities. Unfortunately, cord fibers rot away quickly, leaving no evidence for later generations to study. One of the very few extant firsthand examples of ancient Chinese knotting is the latticework holding together the jade plate-mail suit found in the tomb of the Han Dynasty Princess Tou Wan. Woven in gold thread, it includes little flower-petal knots at the junctures between each small jade plate. These relatively simple knots are quite artistically done, despite the stiffness of the medium in which they are tied. Imagine what the artist could have created with pliable cord.

On the other hand, the jade plate-mail burial suit of the princess reveals little about the use of more commonplace knotwork. References from literary works of two post-Han Dynasty states fill in that gap. Both refer to the "true lover's knot," purported to have been tied in an endlessly repeating pattern and symbolizing, of course, romance and affection. The first ruler of the early sixth century state of Liang, Wu Ti, mentions the knot in a poem about the object of his adoration: "I dreamed the silk cords at our waists/Were bound together in a true lover's knot."

Towards the end of the sixth century, the "true lover's knot" appeared in the Sui Dynasty, the brief unification that foreshadowed the Tang Dynasty. There, as recorded in the official dynastic history, Sui ruler Wen Ti's young concubine Hsuan Hua attracted the admiration of Wen Ti's son and successor, Yang Ti. When Yang Ti ascended the throne, he wished to express his pent-up feelings. Unable to broach the subject directly, Yang Ti turned to the "true lover's knot." He sealed several of them in a gilded box, and ordered it delivered to Hsuan Hua. The message was clear: She was the object of Yang Ti's affection, and he wished to demonstrate his amorous feelings. Although we have no idea how the "true lover's knot" was tied, it is obvious from these examples that knots were replete with symbolic connotations that allowed for extra-lingual communication centuries ago in China.

The "true lover's knot" continued to enjoy widespread use, even finding its way into the titles of two popular melodies of the subsequent Tang Dynasty. The original lyrics are gone, leaving only the title and a hint of the rhythm. But it is a safe guess to assume that the "true lover's knot," and a variety of other knots as well, were known to almost every man and woman in the street by that time.

Even more significantly, Tang sculpture has preserved the designs of a handful of rather complex knots, ones that have survived to the present day. A swastika knot, designed after the ancient Indian motif which Buddhists hold as a symbol of all good fortune, hangs from the waist of a statue of the Goddess of Mercy in the Nelson Gallery of the Atkins Museum in Kansas City, Missouri. A string of knots, including the swastika knot and two simpler ones, can be seen decorating the back of a sash on a Tang tri-color figurine housed in the Royal Ontario Museum in Toronto.

Decorative knotting played an important role in the lives of these early Chinese, both as an aesthetic embellishment in personal attire and as a visual symbol of love and affection or religious concepts. The tying of these knots was long ago considered a necessary skill for all young

A butterfly knot and a good luck knot variation gracing a fan from the Ching Dynasty.

unmarried women to master. The techniques were passed down orally from grandmother to mother to daughter, right along with spinning, weaving, and sewing. Sadly enough, the very nature of this folk craft precluded traditional scholarly attention. Knots were a mundane part of life, a skill common to most women that was surely not worthy of explication in serious classical treatise. The silence is staggering.

Fortunately, the advent of popular vernacular novels in later days opened the avenue for making incidental references to the marginal arts, decorative knotting included. These novels depict ordinary life with an eye for painstaking detail. Here and there, an occasional reference to knotting appears in these works, shedding a few rays of light on the art and its practice.

Striking among these passages is an extended conversation about decorative knots in chapter 35 of the *Dream of the Red Chamber.* There, Pao-yu has summoned Ying-erh to his quarters to ask her to tie a few knotted tassels for him. During their discussion, Ying-erh divulges a host of information: where the knots can be used, the selection of the proper color of cord, a hint at the amount of time needed to tie the knots, and a list of those she is able to tie. The knots in her repertoire bear such fanciful names as the incense knot, the sunflower knot, the plum blossom knot, the elephant's eye knot, the willow leaf knot, and the double diamond knot. These tantalizing names actually tell us little of the designs of the knots; the only one that has survived is the double diamond knot. Nevertheless, the passage demonstrates the wide variety of purely decorative knots in use during the Ching Dynasty.

But by the later Ching, we no longer have to rely on secondhand references. A fine selection of Ching knotwork survives today, housed in the National Palace Museum in Taipei. There are many complex and exquisite Ching knots gracing tassels attached to a host of objects — chops, fans, scepters, sachets, and even eyeglass cases. Even more impressive are knotted *liu su*, large composite hangings made of many knots tied in a multitude of shapes — dragons, carp, phoenix, and cranes, to name a few. The design of these *liu su* is strikingly reminiscent of the jade belt ornaments surviving from the 12th century B.C. The only difference is that the small carved pieces of jade have been replaced with intricate knots. In the Ching Dynasty, these *liu su* decorated large pieces of furniture or accented interior architectural design, hanging from bed canopies, sedan chairs, terrace gables, and the like. Often tied by single girls for their trousseaus, these extravagant medleys required a high degree of skill. Their technical execution, along with the preservation of ancient motifs and designs, leaves no doubt that they were the culmination of a tradition dating back to ancient times.

The decorative knotting tradition continued into the early days of the Republic. But the flood of Western science and technology in this century has changed our lifestyles. In the rush to modernize, we seem to have ignored the traditional arts and crafts. Furthermore, the availability of mass-produced trinkets made handmade knotwork obsolete. The art of knotting was on the verge of extinction.

A decade ago, the only people in Taiwan who knew anything about traditional decorative knotting were a handful of senior citizens and curio dealers. Then, in 1976, a series of articles appeared in ECHO Magazine, one of which explained how some of the simple knots were tied. From this humble beginning, a few creative spirits and cultural afficionados began to try their hands at it. Chinese knotting regained a precarious hold on life.

Today, knotting is again becoming a widespread hobby, as people are rediscovering the relaxation, artistic satisfaction, and beautiful personalized ornamentation it can offer. In addition to learning and sharing the techniques of tying the knots of old, some practitioners are inventing new ones and experimenting with a broad range of new materials — cotton, hemp, durable synthetic fibers, leather, and even fishing line. This promises to add a new and exciting dimension to this ancient craft.

Still, the allure of yesteryear lingers. For the tying of a decorative Chinese knot is much more than a personal endeavor. It is a tribute to Chinese patience, dedication, and ingenuity. And who is to say that knotting the age-old symbols cannot lend a bit of traditional auspiciousness and inner peace to our hectic modern lives?

A knot hanging from a fan held by a character in the *Dream of the Red Chamber.*

INSTRUCTIONS FOR TYING THESE KNOTS ARE ON PAGE 96.

GETTING STARTED

The fundamental skills you will need for tying Chinese decorative knots are presented in the following pages. To begin with, I'll talk about knotting materials and implements and the three basic steps in the knotting process — tying the knot, tightening the cord, and adding the finishing touches. These general guidelines apply to every knot in the book, and should give you a firm foundation on which to build sound knotting skills.

Following that, you will find a guide to the illustrated instructions, which explains the diagrams and the terminology used for all the basic and compound knots. Then the knots themselves are presented in three progressive categories, which have been color coded for easy cross reference. The basic knots, the building blocks of all knotting, have green step-by-step drawings and thumb tabs. The compound knots, combinations and variations of the simple knots, have orange step-by-step drawings and thumb tabs.

Finally, I have selected 41 compositions of varying difficulty, each of which is made up of knots introduced earlier. The drawings show you what the finished products will look like, and the instructions explain the tying process in detail. Though these may appear foreboding at first glance, the drawings and the detailed instructions should allow you to proceed with no problems if you have mastered the basic and compound knots. You'll be surprised at what you can do with a few simple techniques and a little patience and determination.

IMPLEMENTS & MATERIALS

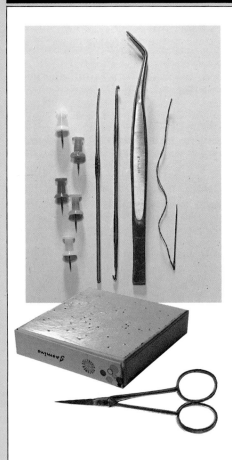

There are literally hundreds of types of cord to choose from — silk, cotton, hemp, jute, synthetic fiber, metal wire, leather, twine, string — in fact, anything at all that can be tied. Don't be fooled into thinking you can only use cords made in China to tie these knots. You can find just what you need almost anywhere in the world, whether it's Taipei, New York, Toronto, or Hillsboro, Illinois. Just look for stores that deal in crafts, yarn, embroidery, tailor's supplies, macrame, or even fishing gear.

Actually, I prefer U.S.-made cord to the local varieties. Of course, if you're a stickler for bone-deep authenticity, you can always find a way to import cords from Taiwan or Hong Kong, but there is really no need. You'll find just what you want in your own neighborhood.

When selecting your cord, pay attention to its stiffness. A rigid cord is hard to control — it just will not conform to shape. On the other hand, an overly pliable cord will not take on any shape at all. Something in between is best for the beginner, and it also helps to use a round cord about half-a-centimeter thick when you are learning the basic knots.

Knots tied in synthetic cord, especially the elastic varieties, tend to slip out of shape very easily. Knots in cotton cord, hemp, or some other material with friction, will hold their shape more easily.

The two-ply flat cord, like the one I used for the following necklace and pendant, can be used to an especially pleasing effect, highlighting the design of the knot and lending it an intricate regularity. But the beginning knotter may have a lot of trouble making it lie flat and avoiding unsightly twists. A round cord is much easier to work with until you get the hang of it.

The choice of cord color, thickness, and pattern, of course, depends entirely on your own artistic instincts. But I would advise against knotting with intricately woven, unevenly tex-

In the old days, people used nothing but their bare fingers to hold the cord in place while tying even the most complicated of knots. But I've found that a few simple tools help keep everything in order.

Using push pins to anchor the cord to a cardboard box or a piece of corkboard will help you follow the pattern as you tie the knot. A crochet hook or a pair of tweezers can help weave the cord through cramped spaces.

For those finishing touches, you'll need a pair of scissors for trimming and needle and thread for touch-ups.

Selection of cord type and color can dramatically change the effect achieved, even in similar compositions.

tured, or variegated cord. You will find that the cord detracts attention from your knots and muddies their patterns.

There are dozens of types of beads, pendants, and other trinkets with which you might want to decorate your knots. They come made of nearly anything — clay, metal, jade, glass, tile, you name it. Whether they are threaded onto the cord itself or sewn on after the knot is done, I find adding these extras is a nice way to accent the beauty of many of the knots.

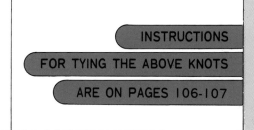

INSTRUCTIONS
FOR TYING THE ABOVE KNOTS
ARE ON PAGES 106-107

TYING

When I first started tying knots, I learned the hard way that it's better to use a little too much cord than to run the risk of coming up short in the end. A three-meter length of cord should be more than enough to tie any one of the basic knots that follow.

It helps a great deal to seal off the ends of the cord before you begin tying, to prevent fraying and unravelling. You can do this in a number of ways — binding the ends with tape or thread, for example, or dipping them in liquid glue or hot wax and letting them set.

Then just lay out the cord according to the diagrams. Remember that if you have beads or pendants that you want strung onto the knotted cord itself (as opposed to being sewn on), these must be strung on at the appropriate point in the tying process.

Make sure that you maintain the proper relationships between the cord sections. Leave enough space for the cord to pass through as many times as will be required, or you will find yourself so cramped that you will not be able to finish the knot. Here is where your push pins will help, holding the configuration immobile so that you can follow the diagrams without losing your place.

As you entwine the cord around itself, be sure that no unwarranted bends, twists, or kinks develop. As the pattern gets more and more complex, you will find your crochet hook and tweezers invaluable, letting you complete the knot without distorting it.

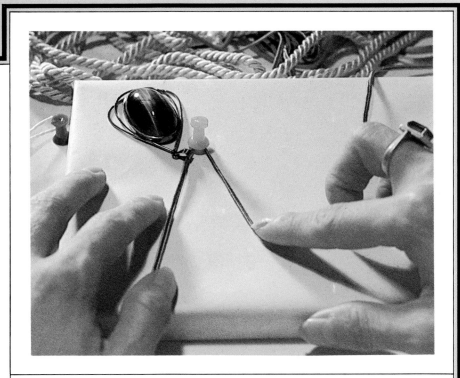

The pendant here will hang from the center of the cord in the finished necklace, so it has to be strung on before the tying begins. Special care must be taken to keep the cord lying flat.

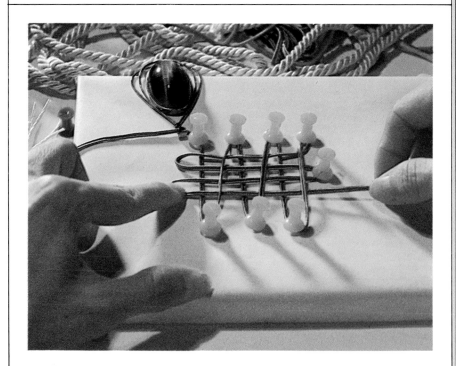

As you lay out the cord in the proper pattern, make sure that the proportions are correct. Using push pins in each of the outer loops will help hold everything securely in place as you continue the knot.

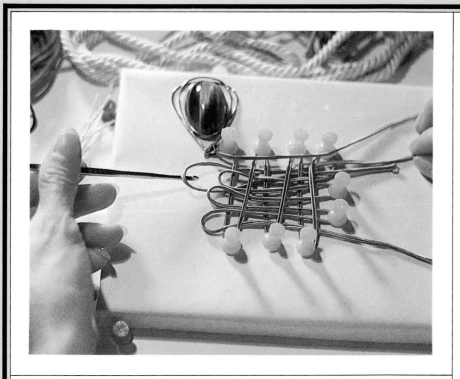

The room to work in gets cramped after a while, and it becomes hard to move one segment of the cord without disturbing others. A crochet hook can help you weave the cord through the tight places without disrupting the pattern.

If you are careful, your knot will be laid out in a perfectly regular pattern, free of kinks and twists. And with enough practice, you will eventually be able to do without the implements, tying the knots right on your hands.

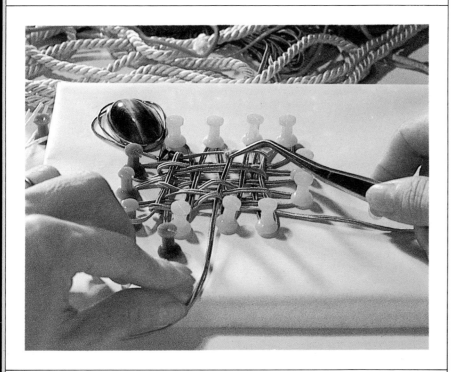

The last steps in tying a knot often entail weaving the cord over and under itself. A pair of tweezers can help you make the cord go where you want it to without twisting it, but be careful not to mar the cord with the sharp edges of the tweezers.

TIGHTENING

Now that the cord has been laid out in the proper pattern, you have to tighten the knot to fix its shape. This is the most critical part of knotting, and haste or impatience can be disastrous.

First, determine which cords are to be pulled, according to the small black arrows in the diagrams. Administer a gentle, even pressure, again making sure that no kinks or twists develop as you go. Tighten the body of the knot completely first.

When the knot has been tightened, you can begin to pull out the slack in the outer loops. Before you start, take a little time to study the knot, mentally tracing the path of the cord before you actually begin pulling on it. Then start from the same point where you began tying the knot, working the slack out loop by loop until you reach the cord ends. But be careful not to let the body of the knot loosen, or its shape will be distorted. If a kink develops, work it out gently by twisting the cord between the thumb and forefinger.

How the knot is tightened will determine the final form it will take. You must control the size of every loop. Adjust them however you want, keeping in mind the knot's overall design. But take care as you pull out the slack; I have found that there is no such thing as too much patience or caution.

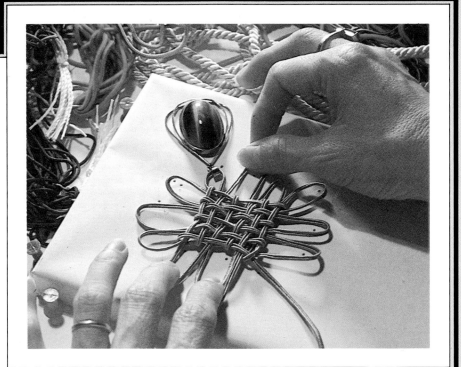

Once the knot is tied, remove the pins and begin tightening. Pull gently and evenly on the outer loops on opposite sides of the knot, tightening the center of the knot first.

Before you take out the slack in the outer loops, study the path the cord weaves through the knot. Then begin at the center of the cord, pulling the slack through loop-by-loop, first in one direction, then in the other.

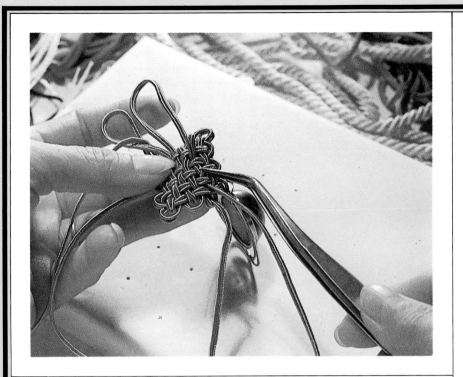

The further you go, the harder it becomes to pull the slack in the loops through without causing twists in the cord. Tweezers will help straighten out unwanted twists without distorting the knot.

Author Lydia Chen

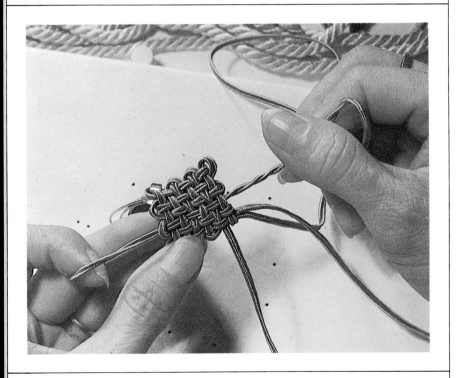

You can take a twist out of the cord while running the slack out. Hold the twisted loop secure, and twirl the other end of the cord in the direction opposite of the twist. The twist will disappear as the cord slides through.

Tightening is the most crucial step in Chinese knotting. It spells the difference between a symmetrical knot and a twisted lumpy mess. Once you have mastered the basics, you will find that slight changes in your tightening technique will lend subtle differences to the character of your knots.

FINISHING

Once the knot has been completely tightened, a few stitches should be made at points which tend to loosen — for example, the corners and the pendant junctures — so that the knot will retain its shape permanently. I try to sew these stitches delicately and discreetly, in thin thread the same color as the cord.

A few small decorative beads may be sewn onto the cord to add to the beauty of the knot. An especially attractive place is within the loops of the knot, as the beads will then highlight the knot's design. But you can sew them on wherever you see fit.

Your composition can be closed off by tying a small tight knot at the end, such as the double connection knot or the button knot. The two loose ends may then be dealt with in a number of ways. You can tie them into a small knot, like the button knot, that will allow the ends to disappear within. You can bind the ends together with thread so that they will not split or unravel. Or, if your creation ends in a large knot like the *pan chang*, you can weave the loose ends back into the body of the knot.

Although these final touches are far less complicated than the other steps, they can really spell the difference between an ordinary decoration and a knotted work of art. I find that the little something extra can really bring a knot to life. Besides, who wants to ruin it after coming this far?

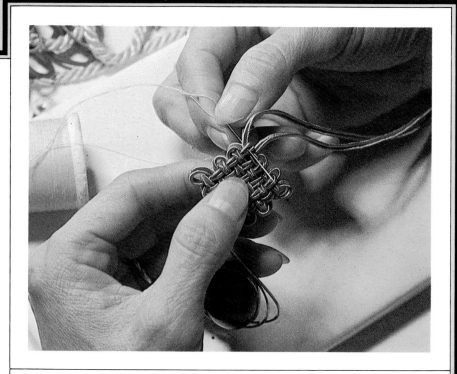

A few stitches at the base of the knot will keep it from slipping out of shape. You should also take some stitches at the opposite corner, where the pendant is hung.

These two tiny beads, sewn carefully into the outer corner loops of the knot, will bring out the full beauty of its pattern. Remember to use thread the same color as the cord, and take your stitches discreetly.

Thread a large bead onto the cord ends, and tie a small double connection knot above it. This little knot will hold the bead and the large knot below it securely in place.

You can finish the necklace by tying a button knot, and then tying each separate end off with a two-loop cloverleaf knot. Don't forget to bind the loose ends to the cords with thread.

The necklace and pendant combination is finished and ready to wear. Like many of the knotted compositions in this book, it is actually quite simple to make. All you need is a little patience and lots of practice.

GUIDE TO THE INSTRUCTION PAGES

Each of the 11 basic knots and 14 compound knots in this book has a set of step-by-step illustrated instructions for you to follow. In order to make them as useful as possible, the guide below details the instructional techniques and reference aids used throughout these two sections.

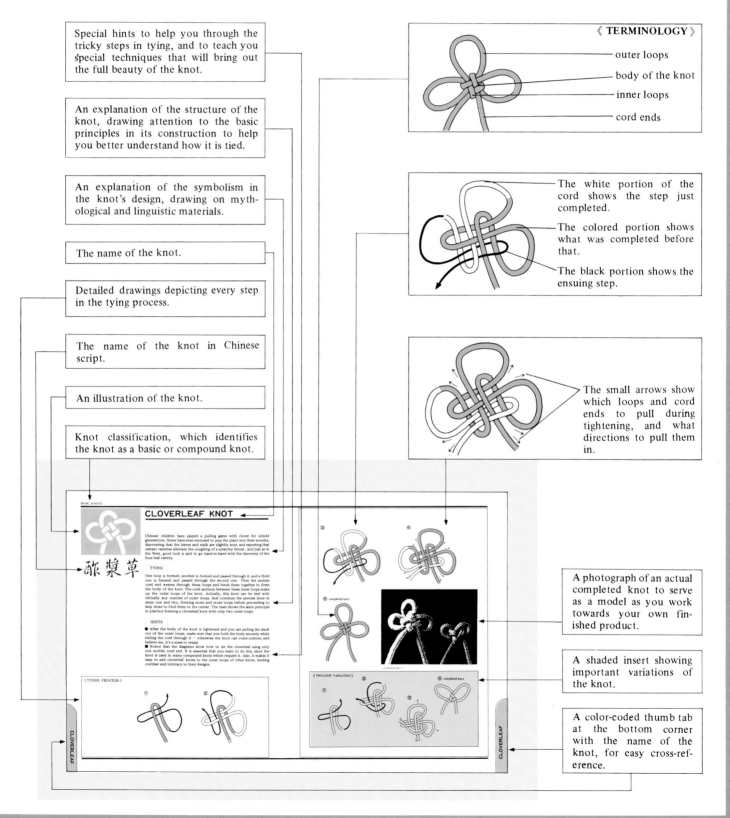

Special hints to help you through the tricky steps in tying, and to teach you special techniques that will bring out the full beauty of the knot.

An explanation of the structure of the knot, drawing attention to the basic principles in its construction to help you better understand how it is tied.

An explanation of the symbolism in the knot's design, drawing on mythological and linguistic materials.

The name of the knot.

Detailed drawings depicting every step in the tying process.

The name of the knot in Chinese script.

An illustration of the knot.

Knot classification, which identifies the knot as a basic or compound knot.

《 TERMINOLOGY 》
— outer loops
— body of the knot
— inner loops
— cord ends

The white portion of the cord shows the step just completed.

The colored portion shows what was completed before that.

The black portion shows the ensuing step.

The small arrows show which loops and cord ends to pull during tightening, and what directions to pull them in.

A photograph of an actual completed knot to serve as a model as you work towards your own finished product.

A shaded insert showing important variations of the knot.

A color-coded thumb tab at the bottom corner with the name of the knot, for easy cross-reference.

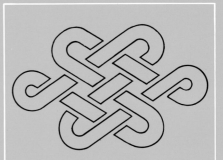

BASIC KNOTS

Until now, Chinese decorative knotting has been an oral tradition. The techniques were handed down from generation to generation. Some have been lost altogether, and the origins of others are shrouded in obscurity. But on the basis of my study with a few of the aged keepers of the tradition and careful analysis of the extant knotwork of old, I have attempted to reduce the techniques used in Chinese decorative knotting, as we now know it, to eleven basic knots.

Some of these knots are clearly representations of traditional auspicious symbols. Others are merely technical devices used in larger knotted pieces. But each of them embodies principles that are used throughout the craft. So even though it might go slowly the first time you tie some of these knots, I recommend that you tie each one several times. Familiarity with each of the basic knots will greatly facilitate tying the more complicated compound knots and creative applications that follow.

The eleven basic knots, in the order in which they appear, are: the double coin knot, the double connection knot, the sauvastika knot, the cross knot, the cloverleaf knot, the good luck knot, the button knot, the *pan chang* knot, the round brocade knot, the plafond knot, and the flat knot.

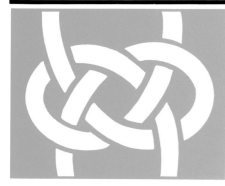

DOUBLE COIN KNOT

The double coin knot is a knotted representation of an often-employed decorative motif, composed of two antique Chinese coins overlapping one another. Merchants once took the design to mean prosperity, hanging it over the entrances to their shops hoping to attract wealth. Used elsewhere, the double coin motif connotes not only prosperity, but longevity as well.

TYING

In tying the double coin knot, two loops are made, one above the other. Then a third loop is made, weaving through the other two to hold them together. The final knot should not be tightened too much. Leave plenty of space within it to bring out its pattern.

HINTS

● This is a very loose knot. I've found it necessary to stitch it together where the cord crosses over itself to keep it from slipping out of shape.
● To tie this knot with one free cord end, simply form two overlapping loops, and weave the end back through their center. Notice that if your second loop lies on top of the first, the loose end comes out on the top of the knot. If the second loop is formed below the first, the situation is reversed.

《 TYING PROCESS 》

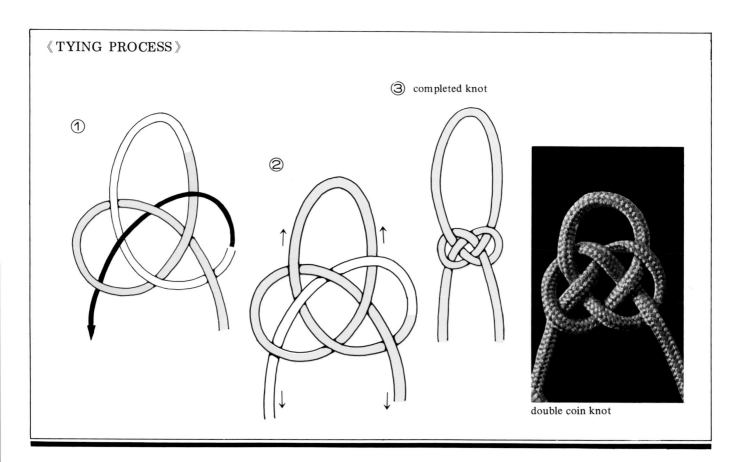

③ completed knot

①

②

double coin knot

DOUBLE CONNECTION KNOT

The double connection knot is exactly what its name suggests — two knots tied into one another. Half of one simple knot forms half of the other.

TYING

In this very stable knot, one cord end is used to tie a simple knot around the other cord end. Then the other cord end is used to tie a simple knot around the first cord end, linking through the loop of the first simple knot. The "x" pattern will appear naturally if the cord is pulled from both top and bottom with equal force.

HINTS

● Keep in mind the desired size of the top loop, or the space between the double connection knot and the one previously tied, as the case may be. These will become much larger than they seem before tightening.

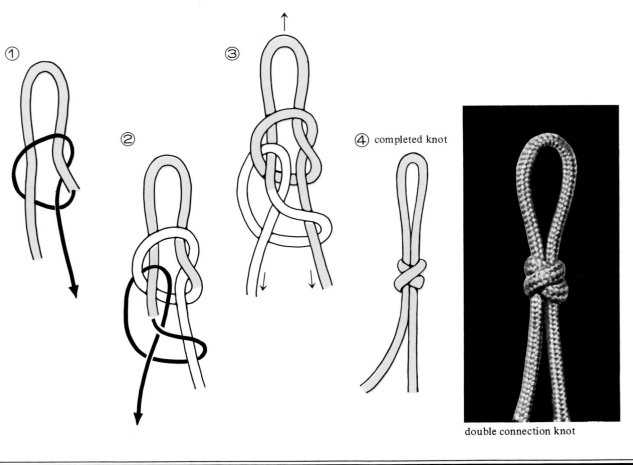

《 TYING PROCESS 》

① ② ③ ④ completed knot

double connection knot

SAUVASTIKA KNOT

The sauvastika, written 卍 , is a sister of the swastika, 卐 , which is familiar in the West as the mark of Hitler's troops and the Nazi Party. Actually both the swastika and the sauvastika are ancient religious motifs with lofty auspicious connotations. They symbolize the Buddha's heart, the seed of Buddhahood in every sentient being's soul, power over evil, and all favor to the good. In China, the symbols were also taken as equivalents for the word "ten-thousand," and early sutra translators sometimes rendered them as "virtue." In Chinese Buddhist symbolism, both the sauvastika and the swastika have come to stand for the accumulation of good fortune and complete virtue, a symbol of Buddhahood and of the Buddha himself.

TYING

A simple knot is tied, and then another, with the second knot hooking through the loop of the first. The cord between the simple knots becomes the top loop, as each of the linked loops is drawn through the center of its opposite knot. When the knot is pulled tight, first horizontally and then vertically, the sauvastika shape will appear naturally.

HINTS

● I've found that this knot is not too stable. You have to pull it quite tight, especially if you are using a synthetic cord. Once the shape is set, you might want to stitch the body of the knot together.

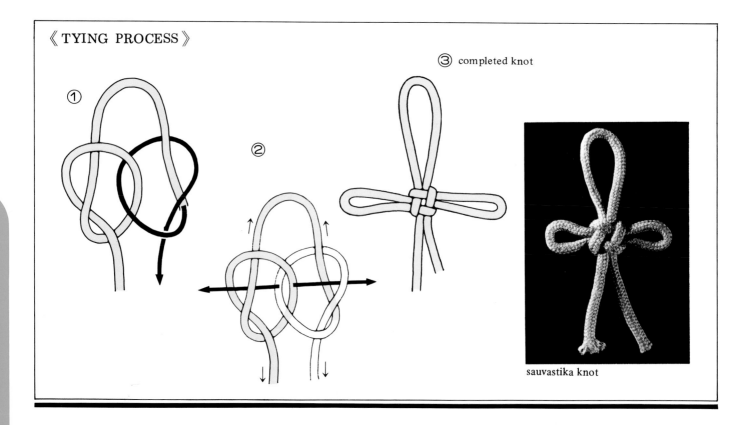

《 TYING PROCESS 》

① ② ③ completed knot

sauvastika knot

SAUVASTIKA

CROSS KNOT

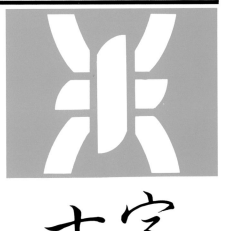

十字

A simple cross in Chinese means "ten," nothing more and nothing less. This knot is tied to look like a cross on one side. On the other side, the cords make a different pattern, something like a four-sided box.

TYING

This knot takes its shape as two "s" curves weave their way into each other to form the body of the knot. It is a very stable knot, and will hold its shape after a minimum of tightening.

HINTS

● You will find that this knot is easy to tie with one cord end, too.

《 TYING PROCESS 》

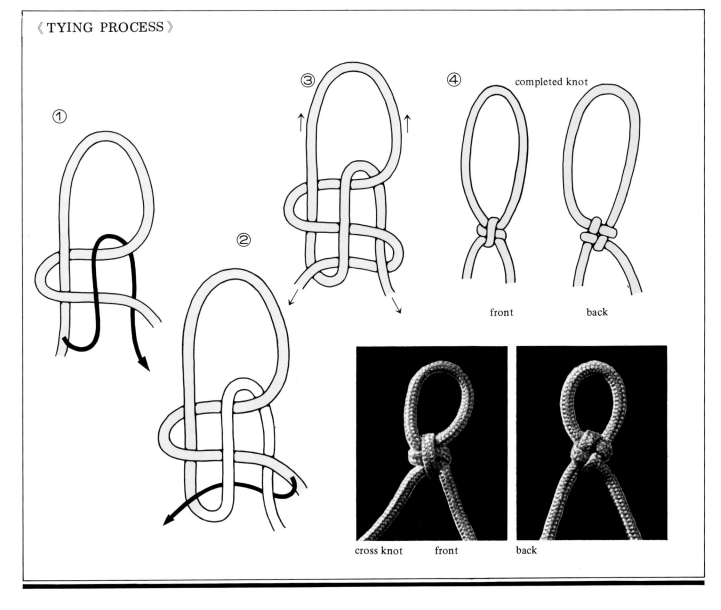

① ② ③ ④ completed knot

front   back

cross knot   front   back

CLOVERLEAF KNOT

Chinese children have played a pulling game with clover for untold generations. Some have even ventured to pop the plant into their mouths, discovering that the leaves and stalk are slightly sour, and reporting that certain varieties alleviate the coughing of a scratchy throat. And just as in the West, good luck is said to go hand-in-hand with the discovery of the four-leaf variety.

TYING

One loop is formed, another is formed and passed through it, and a third one is formed and passed through the second one. Then the mobile cord end weaves through these loops and binds them together to form the body of the knot. The cord sections between these inner loops make up the outer loops of the knot. Actually, this knot can be tied with virtually any number of outer loops. Just continue the process done in steps one and two, forming more and more loops before proceeding to step three to bind them to the center. The inset shows the same principle in practice forming a cloverleaf knot with only two outer loops.

HINTS

● After the body of the knot is tightened and you are pulling the slack out of the outer loops, make sure that you hold the body securely while sliding the cord through it — otherwise the knot can come undone, and believe me, it's a mess to repair.
● Notice that the diagrams show how to tie the cloverleaf using only one mobile cord end. It is essential that you learn to do this, since the knot is used in many compound knots which require it. Also, it makes it easy to add cloverleaf knots to the outer loops of other knots, lending contrast and intricacy to their designs.

《 TYING PROCESS 》

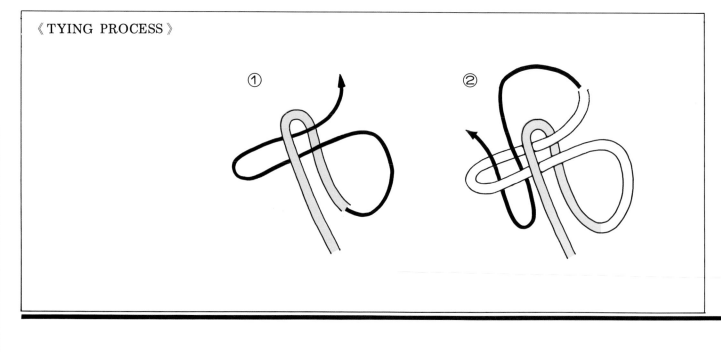

CLOVERLEAF

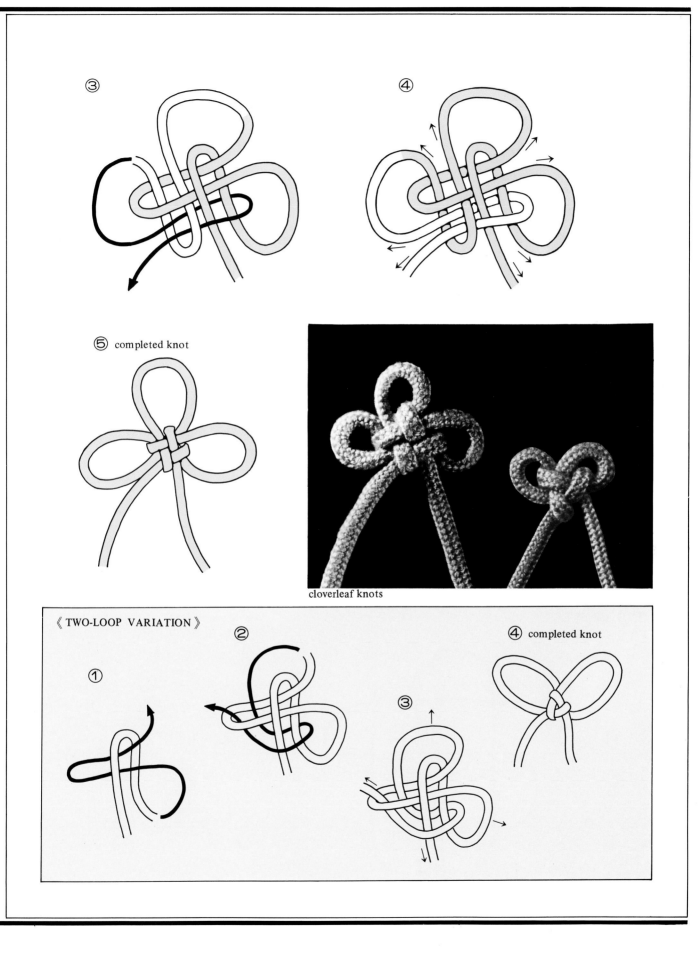

③

④

⑤ completed knot

cloverleaf knots

《 TWO-LOOP VARIATION 》

① ② ③ ④ completed knot

GOOD LUCK KNOT

吉祥

Unlike the majority of knots whose names derive from the decorative motifs they represent, this often-seen knot was a nameless orphan. I have christened it the good luck knot, in keeping with the nomenclature of its many auspicious sister knots. My hope is that it will lend a bit of good fortune to knotter and wearer alike.

TYING

This knot affords almost endless variation. It can be tied with three, four, five, six, or any number of outer loops. If careful attention is paid to the tightening process, it can be tied with compound petals — a small circle of loops in between the large outer ones. To start the knot, lay out the cord with as many elongated loops as you want to appear in the finished product. For reasons of space, the loops in diagrams one, two, and three are not as long as they need to be to actually tie the knot. Cross these loops over each other in the same direction (just like closing a box top), and pull them secure — but not too tight, or the smaller loops will not appear later on. Then repeat the process in the opposite direction. When the knot is finished, the cord ends will be off-center. If you want to hang a pendant off the knot, or proceed with another one, follow alternate steps four and five in the inset to come up with a balanced good luck knot.

HINTS

● It is hard to control the knot when the number of outer loops is more than four or five. I've found that it helps a great deal to stitch them in place before beginning step two. After finishing step two and pulling the cords secure, you can remove the stitches.

《 TYING PROCESS 》

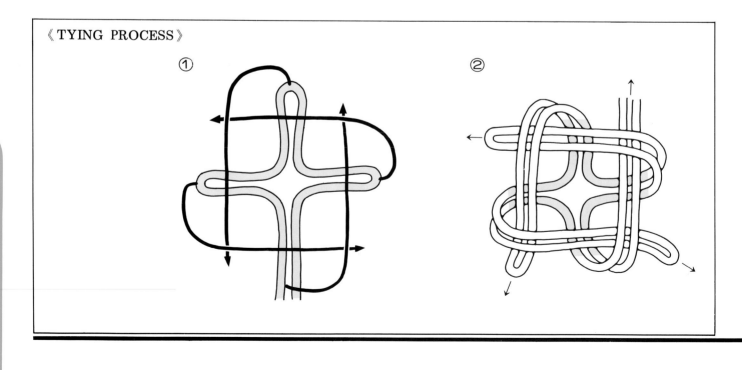

③

④

⑤ completed knot

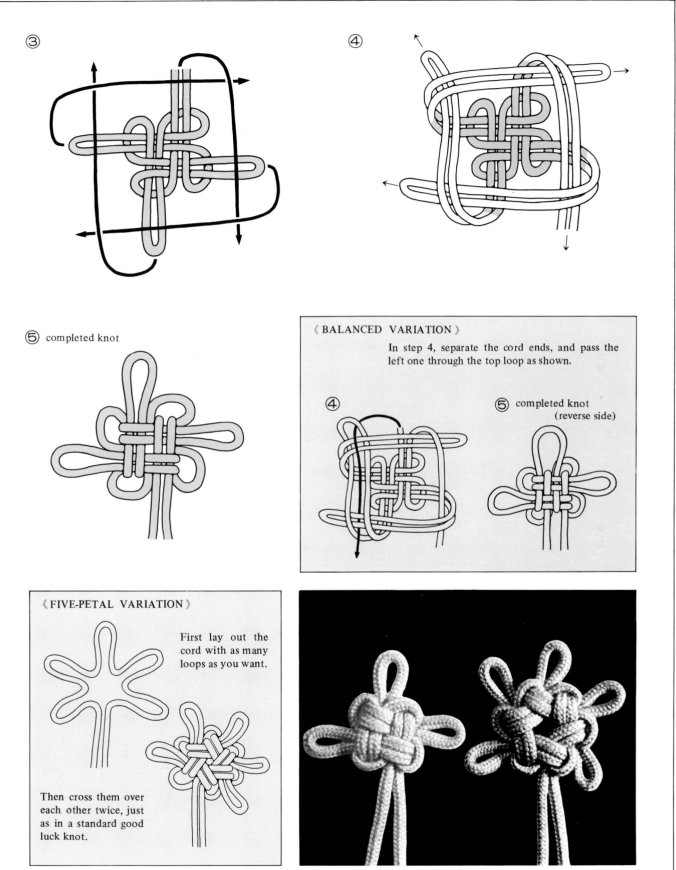

《 BALANCED VARIATION 》

In step 4, separate the cord ends, and pass the left one through the top loop as shown.

④

⑤ completed knot
(reverse side)

《 FIVE-PETAL VARIATION 》

First lay out the cord with as many loops as you want.

Then cross them over each other twice, just as in a standard good luck knot.

good luck knots

鈕扣

BUTTON KNOT

The mystery of those interesting little buttons on traditional Chinese dresses and jackets is rendered commonplace with this simple knot. It can be used in conjunction with other flat-lying knots to make a variety of unusual and attractive clothes fasteners, a sampling of which is shown in the section on creative applications.

TYING

Steps one and two are almost the same as a double coin knot, with the cord going under the last loop on the right instead of over. This cord is then strung over and through the center of the knot in step three. Step four brings the other end of the cord around the left side, through the top loop from underneath, and down through the center of the knot. The knot is tightened in two stages. First, pull the two loose cord ends downward while pushing the knot itself up. Then work out the slack from the upper loop by pulling it through the knot. To make a button knot that lies flat, pull the two loose ends in opposite directions during tightening, as in the inset.

HINTS

● If the knot's shape becomes distorted when it is being tightened, you can remedy it by simply pulling any of the cord segments through the knot in one direction. The shape will reappear as the knot closes.
● Once you have mastered this knot, you should learn how to tie it using only one end of the cord. Many of the later compositions require this.

《TYING PROCESS》

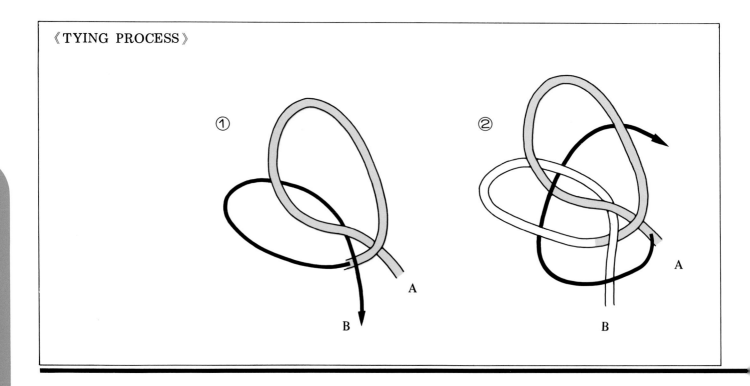

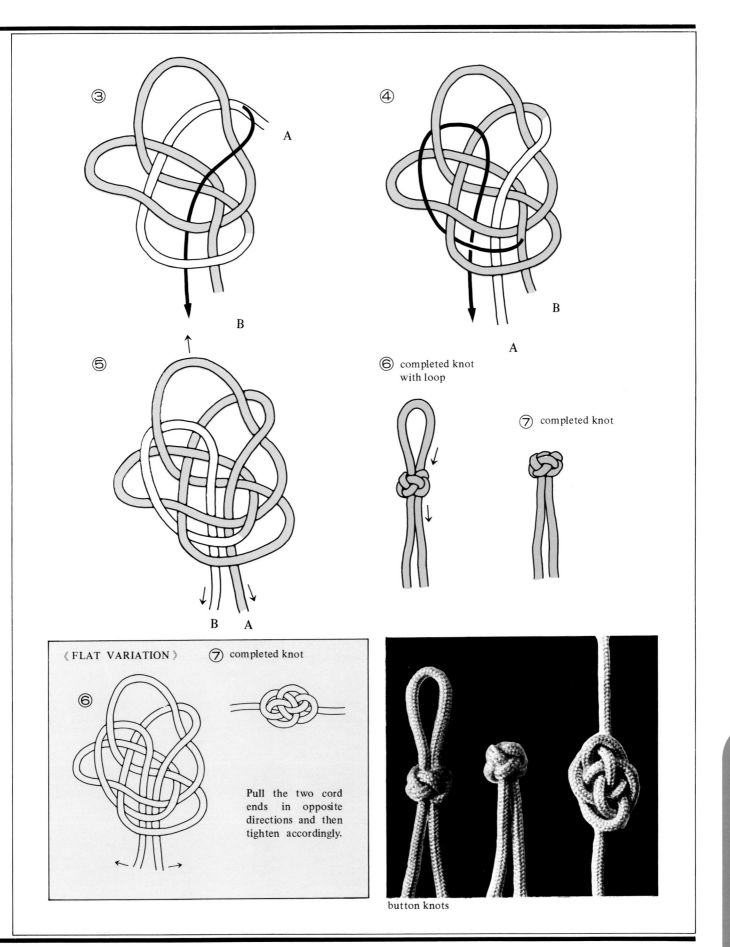

③ A

B

④ B

A

⑤

⑥ completed knot
with loop

⑦ completed knot

B   A

《FLAT VARIATION》 ⑦ completed knot

⑥

Pull the two cord
ends in opposite
directions and then
tighten accordingly.

button knots

盤長

PAN CHANG KNOT

The *pan chang*, or mystic knot, is one of the eight Buddhist treasures. It twists and turns around itself in a seemingly endless pattern, a graphic representation of the cyclical nature of all existence. The *pan chang* knot embodies this concept, one of the basic precepts in Chinese Buddhism.

TYING

In this very stable knot, the cord is woven into a double-thickness square pattern, the warp and woof of which can be increased to make the knot as large as you want. Pay close attention to the weaving done in step three, because an understanding of this will come in handy when you tie any of the many *pan chang* variations. Here, the cord from the corner loop goes under one cord, over three, under one, and over three again. It turns back, goes under two, over one, under three, over one, and under one to form another outer loop before repeating the whole process. Although the specific "overs" and "unders" will not be exactly the same in every variation, the underlying principle is unchanging: on the way up, the cord goes over everything except the pairs of cords that form the inner loops on the edge of the knot's body. Here the mobile cord goes under the first cord of each pair. On the way back down, the pattern is reversed: the cord goes under everything, again except for the pairs that form the inner loops on the left. In these places it goes over the same ones it went over on the way up.

HINTS

● Don't tighten the body of the knot too much, or it will be impossible to take the slack out of the outer loops without distorting the pattern.
● To make sure that the final knot is regularly shaped, and that the two cord ends are the same length, take the slack out starting from the top loop and working in both directions. After you finish in one direction, you might want to turn the knot over so that you can pull the slack through in the other direction with the same hand — this helps ensure that the force applied will be the same in both directions.

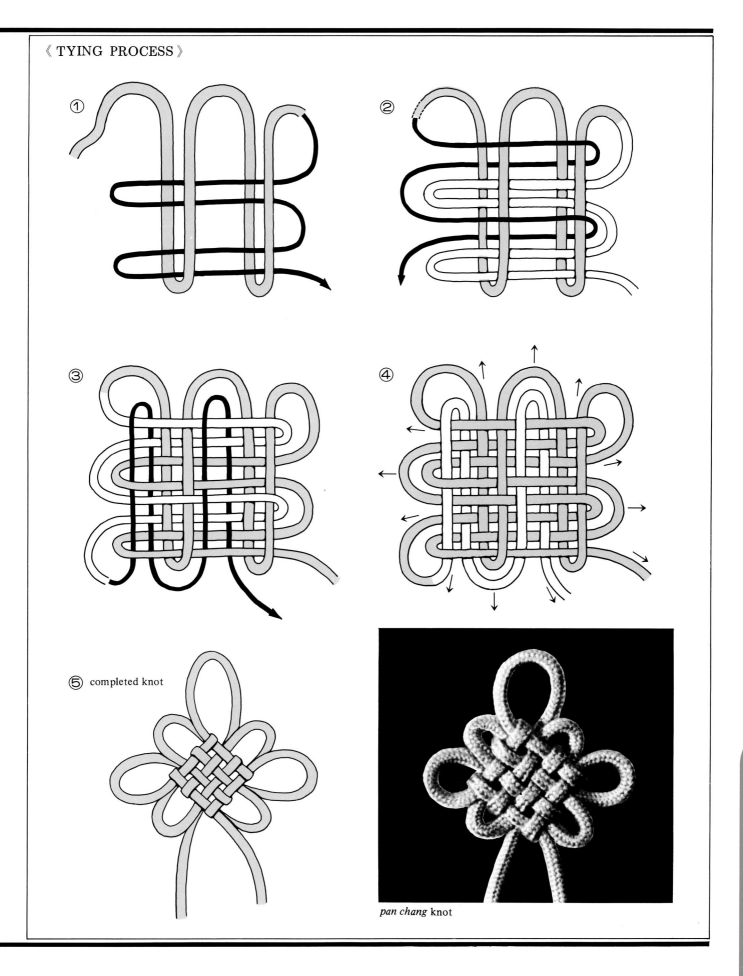

① ② ③ ④

⑤ completed knot

pan chang knot

團錦

ROUND BROCADE KNOT

This knot takes inspiration from rounded patterns often seen in Chinese brocade. A close look at these brocade designs reveals that they are often abstract representations of auspicious animals or characters — the dragon, the crane, the character for longevity, and the like. The fact that they are worked into a round pattern further enhances the message of good fortune, for the circle represents completeness to the Chinese.

TYING

In this knot, the outer loops are bound together by passing through each other's centers in a circular pattern. Cord A makes two horizontal passes, going under everything right to left, and over everything left to right. Then it travels up under everything to pass through the top loop, and down over everything to take its final position. Cord B's travels will be easier to grasp if you imagine the portion of it that comes straight down from the top loop as the knot's spine. After going up through the inner loops on the left, cord B passes through the knot twice horizontally. On each pass, when it travels left to right, it goes over everything except the spine and the cords crossing over and under the spine. When it travels right to left, it passes under every cord except the last two — the ones that it came over to begin the pass, thus returning to its origin.

HINTS

● Notice that cord A forms the top loop and the two on the right, while cord B forms the two on the left, and that the cords always move away from the top of the knot when they form a loop.
● Eventually, for some of the creative applications in the back of the book, you will have to learn to tie this knot using only one mobile cord end. Follow step seven in the drawings, and proceed very carefully.

《TYING PROCESS》

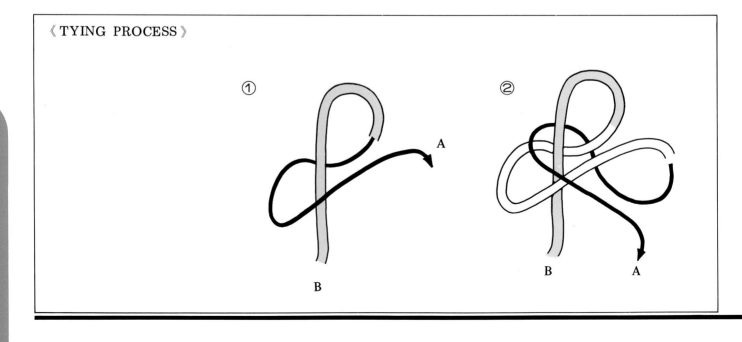

ROUND BROCADE

③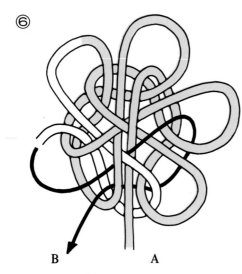

④

⑤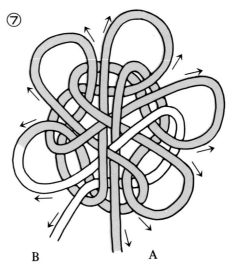

⑥

⑦

⑧ completed knot

round brocade knot

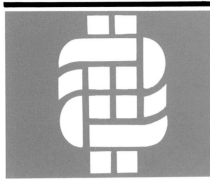

PLAFOND KNOT

藻井

This knot is designed after the grand decorations seen on the center of ceilings in Chinese temples and palaces. The ceilings are divided into nine rectangular sections, three across and three deep. The center section curves away from the floor. A circular design, often composed of auspicious motifs, fills its apex. This is surrounded by a balanced repetition of a complimentary motif that radiates out to the edges of the bordering rectangle. This effect is echoed in the plafond knot, with its spiral-like center and its rectangular border.

TYING

Cord A makes a double horseshoe shape around the original loop, tying a simple knot into itself before coming down to the bottom. Cord B then passes through the bottom of this simple knot, around through the ends of A's horseshoe, under the original loop, and through the top of A's simple knot to make a horseshoe of its own. On its way down, it weaves through the central knot to make a symmetrical pattern.

HINTS

● You will have a lot of trouble if you don't tighten the central knot first. Take the slack out of the outer loops only after the center has been fixed securely in place.

《 TYING PROCESS 》

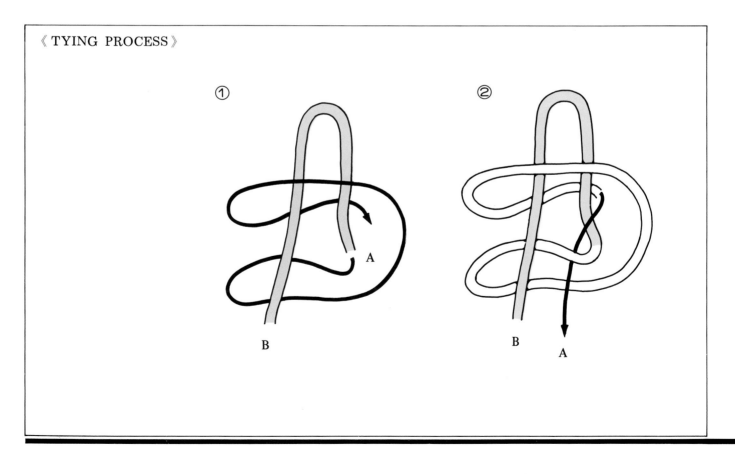

① ②

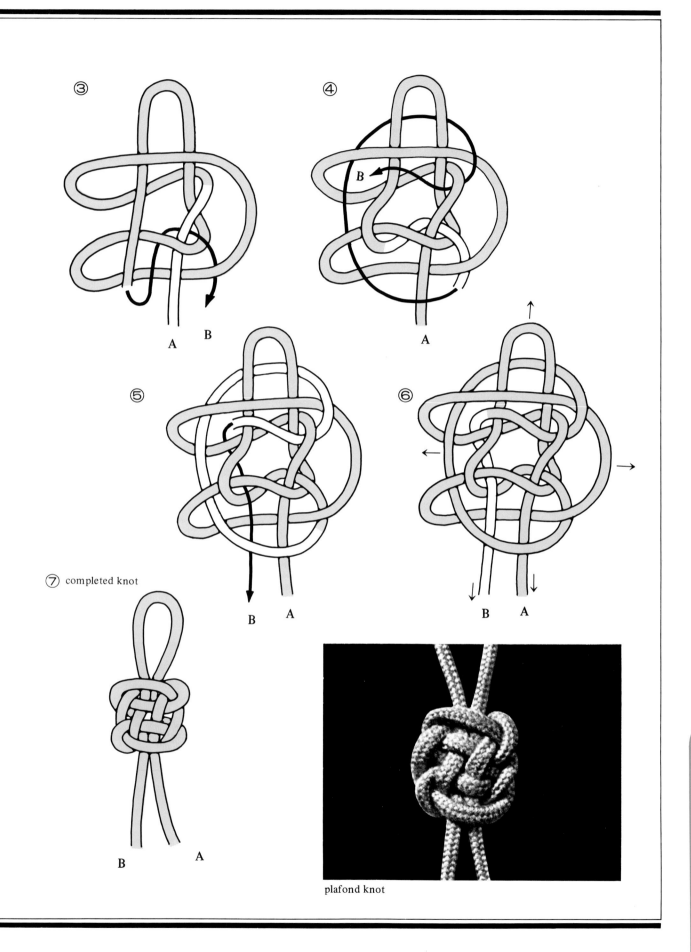

③

④

⑤

⑥

⑦ completed knot

plafond knot

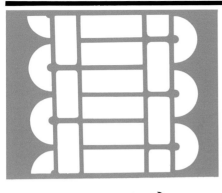

平结

FLAT KNOT

The flat knot, exactly the same as Western macrame's square knot, has had a long history in both China and the West.

TYING

This is a simple knot to tie. First bring the right cord over the axle and under the left cord. Then bring the left cord under the axle and up through the loop on the right. Tighten, then take the new right cord under the axle and over the left cord, and pass the left cord over the axle and down through the loop on the right. Tighten, and repeat for as many knots as you want in the series.

HINTS

● If you tie the second half of each knot exactly the same as the first, the series will spiral around the axle instead of lying flat on one side.

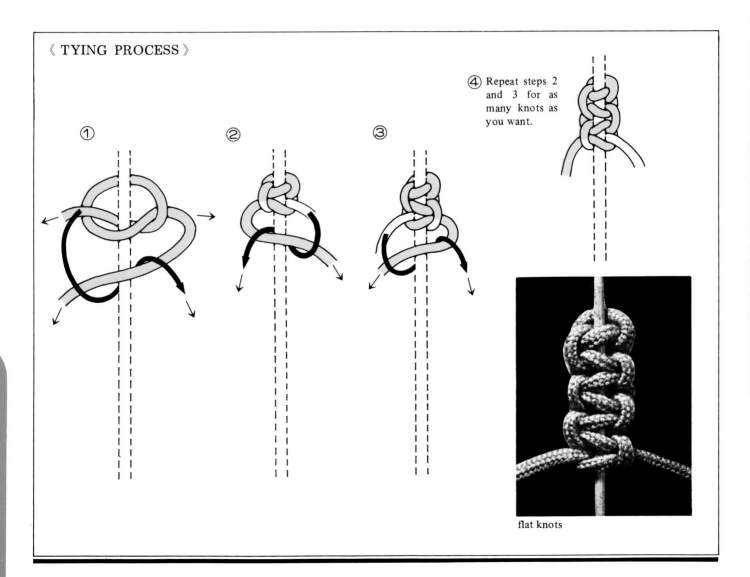

《 TYING PROCESS 》

④ Repeat steps 2 and 3 for as many knots as you want.

①　②　③

flat knots

COMPOUND KNOTS

These 14 knots are either combinations of basic knots or variations of their designs. In them, the basic knots are brought together to form more complex and symbolically significant configurations drawn from Nature, folk imagination, and the Chinese language.

The techniques used to combine and connect the basic knots to form the compound ones are important. While the basic knots lay the groundwork for understanding the structure of the individual knots themselves, the compound knots introduce the principles behind the overall structure of knotted pieces, teaching you the various ways to bring the knots together.

In addition, the combinations are lovely in and of themselves, rich in imagery and aesthetically pleasing to the eye. They make fine decorations independently, and begin to show the wealth of possibilities Chinese knotting has to offer. In the order in which they appear, they are: the *ju i* knot, the brocade ball knot, the longevity knot, the double happiness knot, the dragon knot, the dragonfly knot, the butterfly knot, the long *pan chang* knot, the stone chime knot, the double diamond knot, the crane knot, the phoenix knot, the fish knot, and the ten-accord knot.

JU I KNOT

The *ju i* is an elongated scepter about the length of a back scratcher. Its two rounded ends are flattened and scalloped, which is echoed in this knot. The name *ju i* means "everything according to your heart's desire." Some say that the *ju i* scepter came to China with early Buddhist missionaries, who used a similarly shaped device as a note-taking surface during explications of the sutras. Others assert that the *ju i* is indigenous in origin, pointing to the fact that its rounded ends are strikingly similar to a Taoist motif signifying immortality. Whatever the case may be, the *ju i* is a symbol of great fortune. To carry one is to court good luck, and to own one is to enjoy prosperity.

TYING

The *ju i* is made up of four cloverleaf knots, the one in the center bringing the three outer ones together. First, tie three cloverleaf knots in a series on one cord, leaving them several centimeters apart. Then use the two loops that hang down between them and the two loose cord ends to tie a fourth cloverleaf, the loops of which will run directly into the bodies of the outer knots. Adjust and tighten so that the loops of all four knots are the same size.

HINTS

● Remember not to let the centers of the cloverleaf knots loosen when you are taking out slack. Hold the bodies firmly while running the extra cord through.

● The diagrams show how to tie the *ju i* knot using both ends of the cord. Eventually, some compositions will require you to tie it using only one end. This will mean tying one of the outer cloverleaf knots first, instead of the top one, and tying the center one in stages as you proceed from one outer knot to the top one to the other outer knot.

《TYING PROCESS》

① First tie a clover-leaf knot.

②

③

④ Tie each cord end into a cloverleaf.

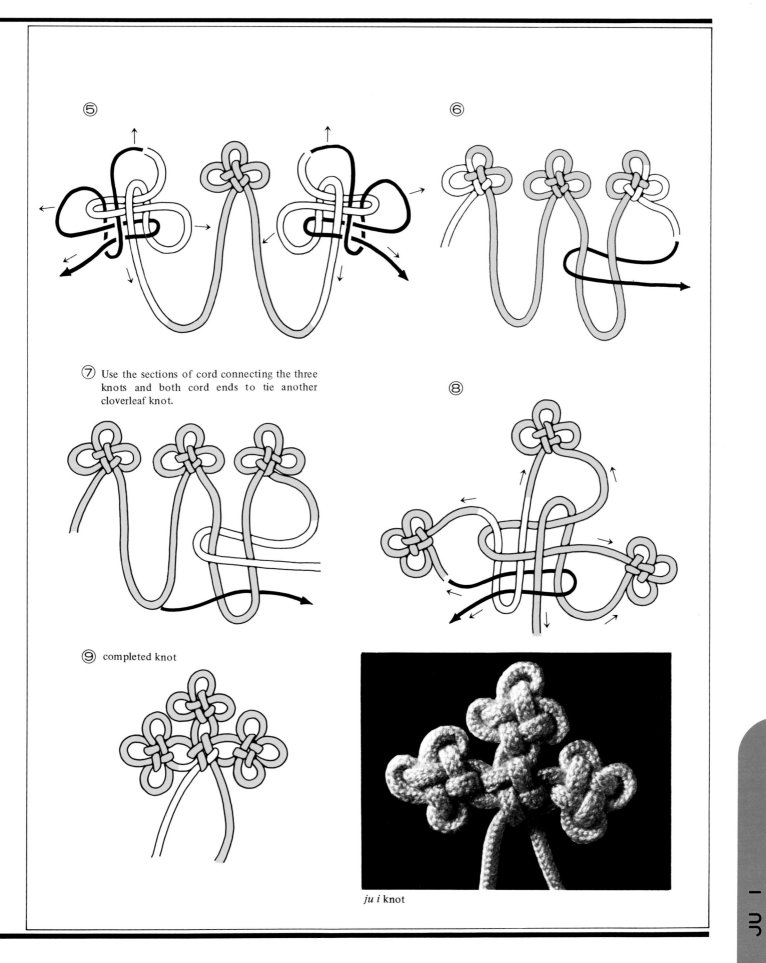

⑤

⑥

⑦ Use the sections of cord connecting the three knots and both cord ends to tie another cloverleaf knot.

⑧

⑨ completed knot

ju i knot

繡球

BROCADE BALL KNOT

As far back as the Tang Dynasty, casting the brocade ball has been synonymous with selecting a husband. The indecisive maid has only to throw the ball into the midst of a group of eager suitors; the man who fields it is on the way to the altar. Fate often knows best, and the Chinese brocade ball is the messenger of preordained conjugal bliss.

TYING

The brocade ball is composed of five cloverleaf knots. Tie three in a series on one cord, but with the adjacent loops linked together. Use the two loops hanging down between them and the loose cord ends to tie a fourth cloverleaf in the middle of the other three. Finally, close off the circle by tying another cloverleaf, again linking its two side loops with the adjacent loops of the other knots.

HINTS

● Make sure that all the loops in the outer circle are the same size.
● Make sure that the loops are linked together in a symmetrical fashion so that the entire brocade ball knot will lie flat.

《 TYING PROCESS 》

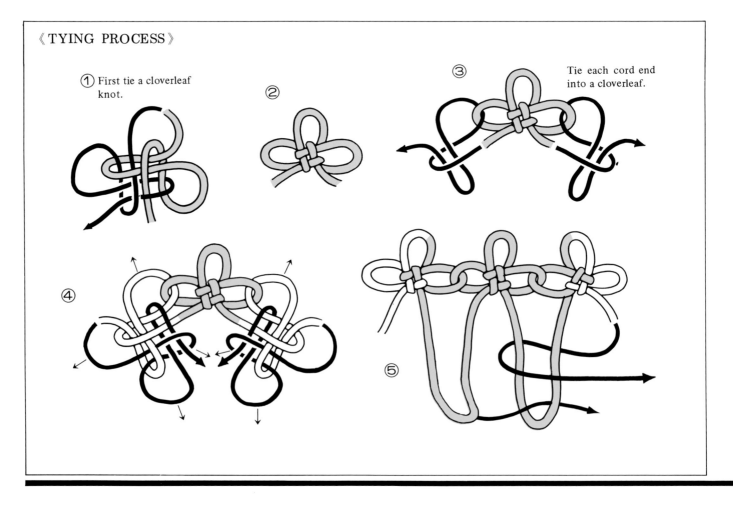

① First tie a cloverleaf knot.

②

③ Tie each cord end into a cloverleaf.

④

⑤

BROCADE BALL

62

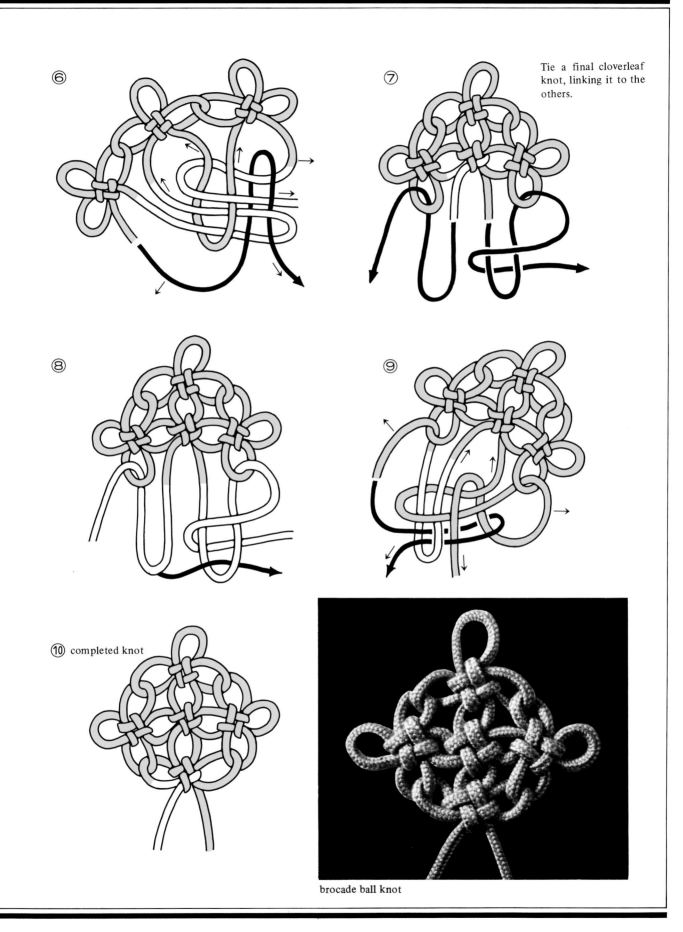

⑥

⑦ Tie a final cloverleaf knot, linking it to the others.

⑧

⑨

⑩ completed knot

brocade ball knot

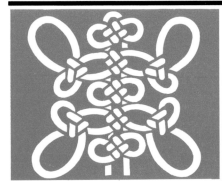

LONGEVITY KNOT

Birthday wishes in Chinese are simple and to the point, and have been for centuries. One character, which means longevity, does the trick. It, and designs based on it, decorate nearly every Chinese birthday card, birthday present, and most birthday cakes and cookies. Throughout the ages, the character has also been rendered in every conceivable script. Two designs from the Ching Dynasty, each containing 100 longevity characters, no two of which are exactly alike, demonstrate the wide range of possibilities in longevity character designs. The longevity knot takes its shape from such slightly abstracted and decorative renditions of the character. Its felicitous message is a universal one -- "may you live a long and happy life."

TYING

The longevity knot is made up of four two-loop cloverleaf knots gracing a column of five standard cloverleaf knots. First tie a three-loop cloverleaf, then tie a two-loop variation on either side of it. Bring these three knots together by means of another three-loop cloverleaf, tied with the two loose cord ends and the two loops hanging between the knots. Tie another three-loop cloverleaf to serve as the center of the knot, and then tie another four-knot configuration that mirrors the one above the center knot.

HINTS

● I have found that if you want to hang something heavy off the end of the longevity knot, you have to stitch it together securely on the reverse side. Otherwise, the weight will cause the knot to slip out of shape.
● If the knot is to serve as an independent decoration, you can hide one of the loose cord ends within the body of the last cloverleaf knot, form the other end into a loop, and hide it in the body as well.

《 TYING PROCESS 》

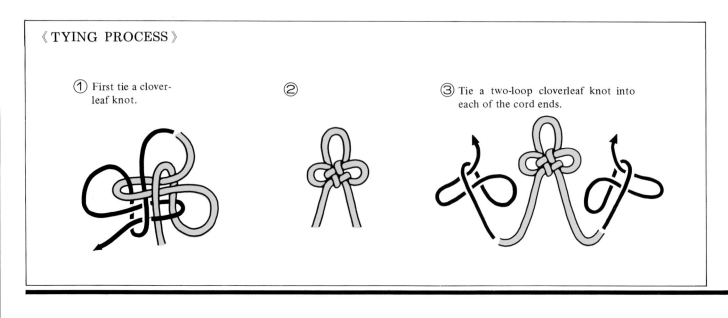

① First tie a clover-leaf knot.

②

③ Tie a two-loop cloverleaf knot into each of the cord ends.

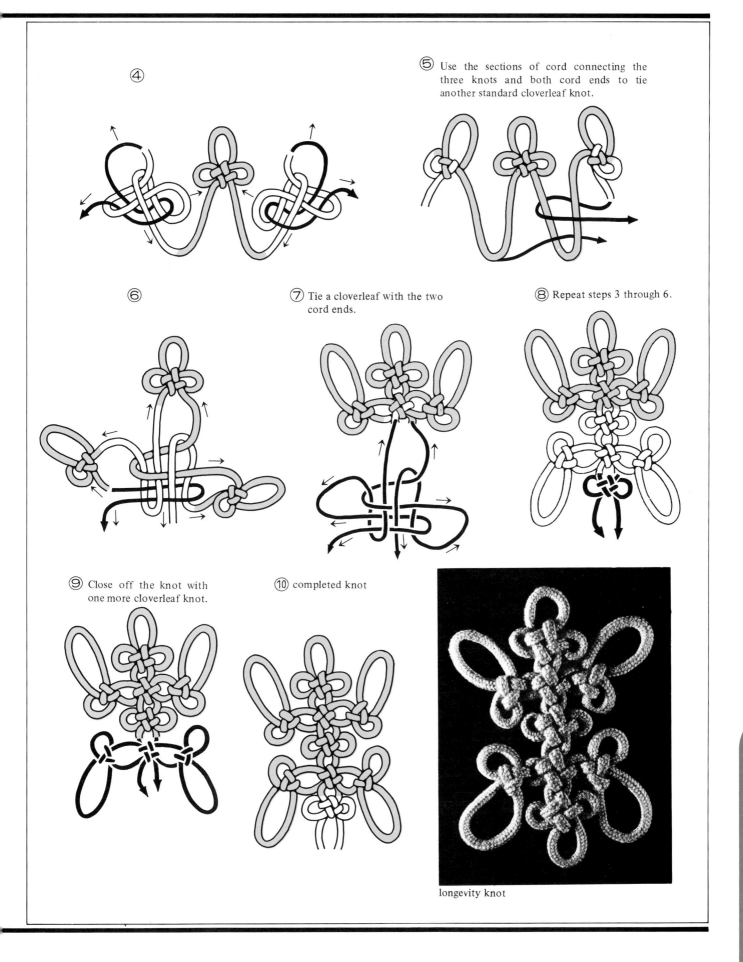

④

⑤ Use the sections of cord connecting the three knots and both cord ends to tie another standard cloverleaf knot.

⑥

⑦ Tie a cloverleaf with the two cord ends.

⑧ Repeat steps 3 through 6.

⑨ Close off the knot with one more cloverleaf knot.

⑩ completed knot

longevity knot

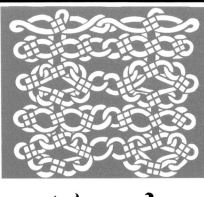

DOUBLE HAPPINESS KNOT

The double happiness emblem, 囍 , is seen at every Chinese wedding. The two happiness characters drawn side by side succinctly and aptly express the joys of matrimony.

> TYING

Two cords are used to tie the double happiness knot. The first is used to tie fifteen cloverleaf knots to form the right half of the emblem. The second repeats the pattern for the left half, linking through the five loops on the adjacent edge of the first half.

> HINTS

● Except for the two top knots, where the loops themselves form lines of the emblem, virtually all the slack should be pulled out of the cloverleaf knots, so that the loops disappear. This will make the lines of the knot resemble the double happiness emblem more closely.
● Make sure that the five connections between the two halves are all linked in the same direction.
● You can hide the four loose ends at the bottom by tucking them into the reverse sides of their knots.

《 TYING PROCESS 》

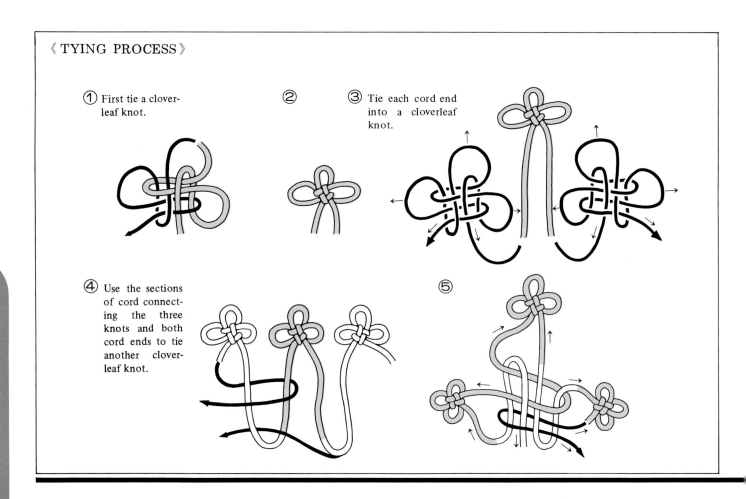

① First tie a cloverleaf knot.

②

③ Tie each cord end into a cloverleaf knot.

④ Use the sections of cord connecting the three knots and both cord ends to tie another cloverleaf knot.

⑤

⑥ Tie another cloverleaf knot.

⑦ Use each cord end to tie another cloverleaf, linking them to the one above.

⑧ Use both cord ends to tie a single cloverleaf knot, linking it to the side ones.

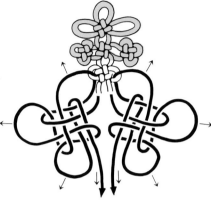

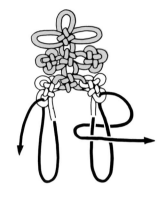

⑨

⑩

⑪ Repeat steps 3 through 10.

⑫ Use another cord to tie a cloverleaf knot, linking it to the first knot you tied.

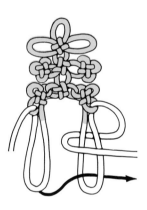

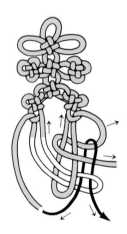

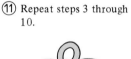

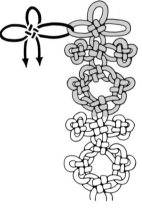

⑬ Repeat steps 3 to 11, linking the knots together at the four points that touch.

⑭ completed knot

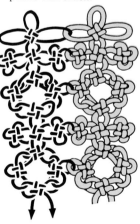

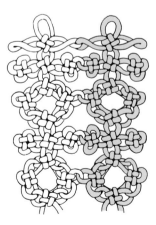

double happiness knot

DRAGON KNOT

The dragon is the symbol most representative of things Chinese. He controls the rain, clouds, thunder, water, and, by extension, fertility. On the purely fantastic side, the dragon has done his best to swell the ranks of the Chinese supernatural menagerie. He once fell in love with a stork and their union produced the phoenix. On a lordly visit to the earth, the dragon became enamored of a fine mare and they bore a unicorn. Since the second century B.C., the dragon has also served as a symbol of Chinese emperors and their power. Practically everything connected with the emperor took on the adjective ''dragon'' — like the dragon countenance, the dragon throne, and the dragon robes. And like the emperor, credited with embodying virtue itself, the Chinese dragon has also come to symbolize all things good: wisdom, justice, benevolence, and just plain good luck.

TYING

The head of the dragon is composed of three two-loop cloverleaf knots. Each of the outer ones is tied with one loose cord end and an existing loop of the center one. All the slack is then taken out, except for the slack in the two uppermost loops, which are to be sewn into the shapes of the mouth and crown. The body can be tied together with many kinds of knots — for example, the double coin knot, or, as here, the double connection knot. The tail is then coiled and sewn into place.

HINTS

● You should make the loop that forms the crown a bit bigger than the one that forms the mouth.
● The completed dragon is not balanced, and so will not hang well. But it can be laid flat, or added to the borders of a centrally oriented composition.

《 TYING PROCESS 》

① First tie a two-loop cloverleaf knot.

②

③

④ Turn the knot so that the loops face down, and use each loop and cord end to tie a two-loop cloverleaf knot.

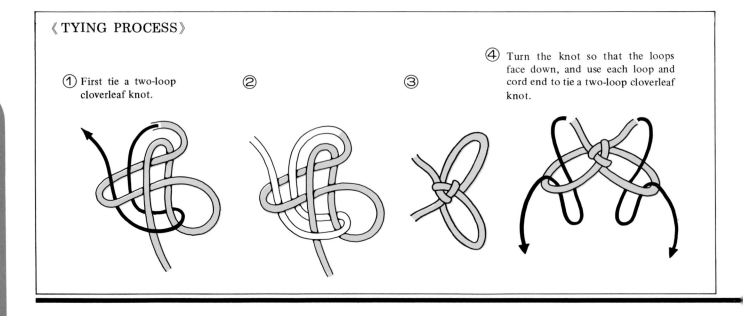

DRAGON

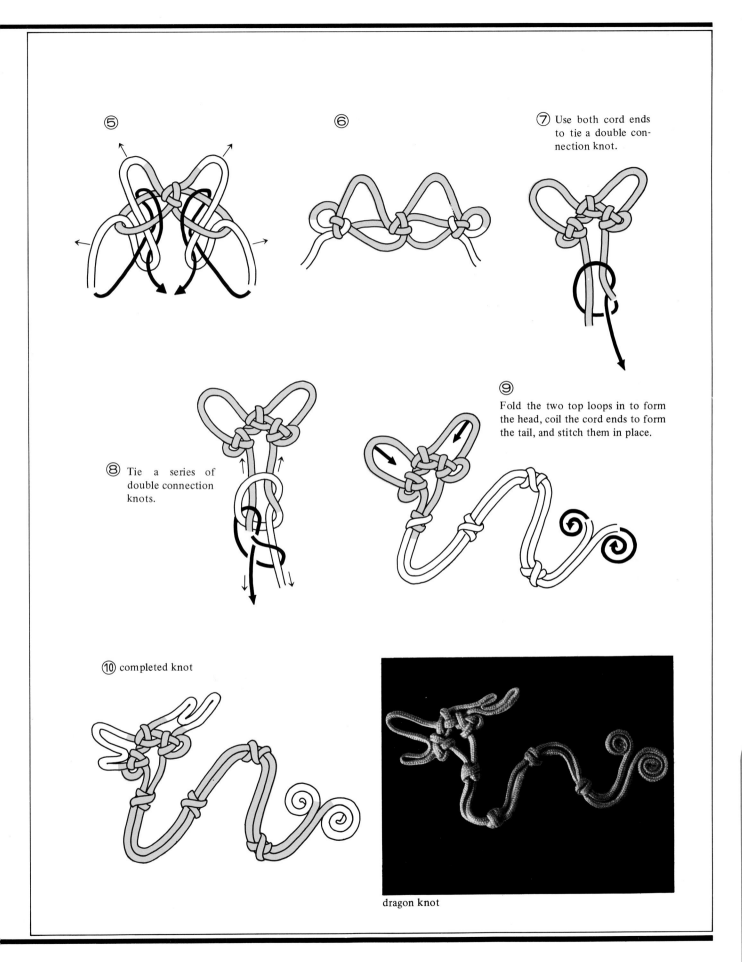

⑤

⑥

⑦ Use both cord ends to tie a double connection knot.

⑧ Tie a series of double connection knots.

⑨ Fold the two top loops in to form the head, coil the cord ends to form the tail, and stitch them in place.

⑩ completed knot

dragon knot

DRAGONFLY KNOT

The dragonfly, though it does not have a rich mythological heritage, has fascinated young and old throughout the ages in China. Children tax their wits to snare them, even chanting a ditty to lure males toward a captive dragonfly maiden. Dragonflies, noted for their speed and agility, can often be seen flittering to and fro near ponds and streams in search of food. Their capricious, erratic flight and the beauty of their lacy wings and orb-like eyes have earned them a special place in the hearts of Chinese artists and poets. Perhaps the artists felt a tinge of envy as they watched the dragonfly's flight, wishing to rid themselves of the constraints of daily intercourse and taste the pleasures of playful abandon.

TYING

Use two cords, tying them as if they were one, to begin the dragonfly knot. First, tie a button knot to serve as the head. After tightening, tie a sauvastika knot just below it. The loops will come out of the sides to form two pairs of wings. Then, use the outer two cord ends to tie a series of flat knots around the inner two to make the body.

HINTS

● Don't let the two cords twist around each other, or your dragonfly's wings will not lie flat.
● If you clip off one of the inner cord ends about halfway down the desired length of the body, the series of flat knots will taper, and form a more lifelike dragonfly.

《 TYING PROCESS 》

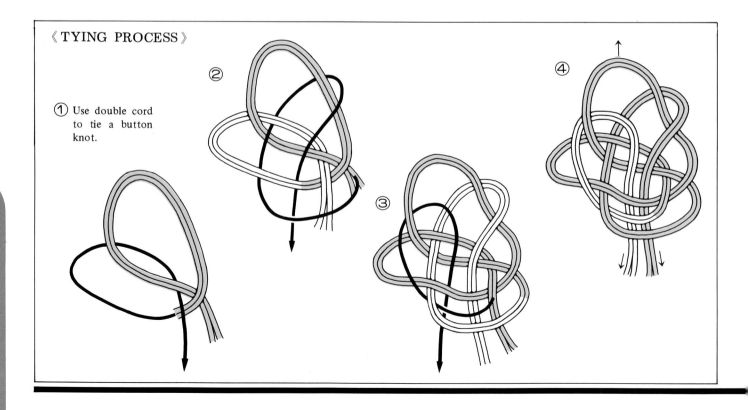

① Use double cord to tie a button knot.

② ③ ④

⑤

⑥

⑦ Use the double cord to tie a sauvastika knot, leaving the side loops long to form the wings.

⑧

⑨ Use the outer two cords to tie a flat knot around the inner two.

⑩ Continue to tie a series of flat knots for the body.

⑪ completed knot

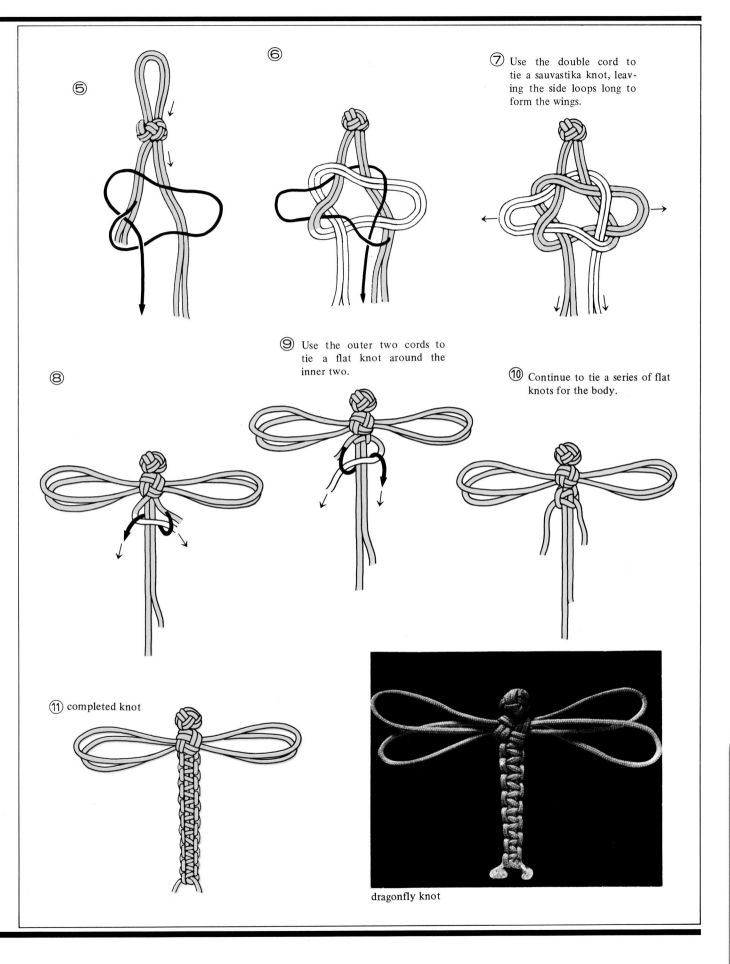

dragonfly knot

蝴蝶

BUTTERFLY KNOT

One night, Chuang Chou dreamt he was a butterfly, flying through the air, totally at ease, and unaware of his existence as a man. But when Chuang awoke, much to his surprise, he found himself still a man. Did Chuang dream that he was a butterfly? Or did a butterfly dream it was Chuang? Or do the very concepts "butterfly" and "Chuang" create arbitrary divisions in the singularity that gives rise to all things? The butterfly in this parable intimates the essential oneness of all being, a basic tenet of Taoist philosophy.

TYING

The body of the butterfly knot is a simple *pan chang* knot. In the course of tying, the cord travels through two of the *pan chang's* outer loops to form a double coin knot at the corner. The process is repeated at the opposite corner. These double coin knots serve as the butterfly's wings, and the remaining outer loops make up the head and the lower wing tips.

HINTS

● Tighten the *pan chang* and double coin knots completely before taking out the slack. When you take out the slack, rotate the double coin knots in opposite directions, so that the two outer loops will be at the top rather than the bottom.

《TYING PROCESS》

① First tie a double coin knot to form one wing.

② Use one loop of the double coin knot and both of the cord ends to start a *pan chang* knot.

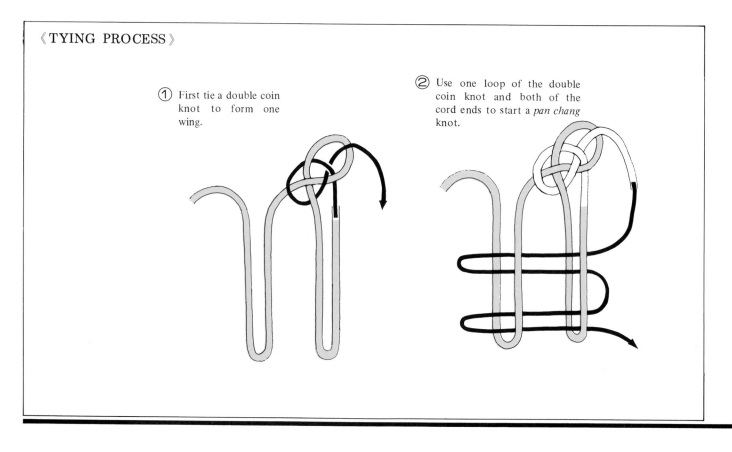

BUTTERFLY

72

③ Now tie another double coin knot that mirrors the first one.

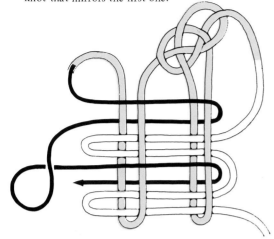

④

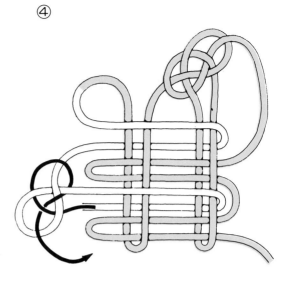

⑤

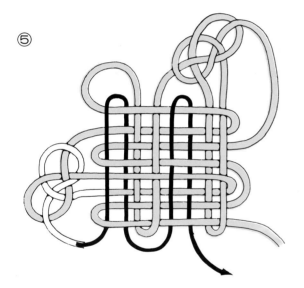

⑥

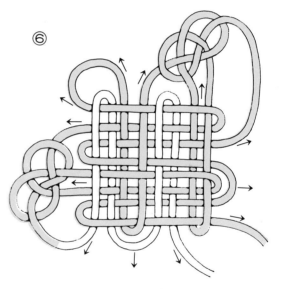

⑦ completed knot

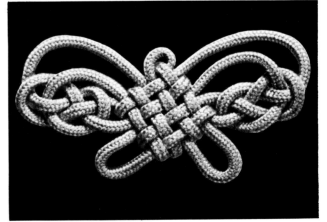

butterfly knot

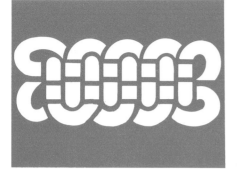

LONG PAN CHANG KNOT

長盤長

If a composition calls for an oblong section of knotting, use this variation of the *pan chang.* The long *pan chang,* a horizontal complement to other surrounding knotwork, hangs balanced at its center.

TYING

The basic pattern laid out in steps one, two, and three is the same as that of the regular *pan chang,* except that there are more vertical loops and fewer horizontal ones. The weaving in step four is done with both cord ends, to allow them to meet in the center of the rectangle rather than in a corner. As in the standard *pan chang,* the inner loops form the edge of the body of the knot. The pattern here is under one and over three on the way up; under two, over one, and under one on the way back down.

HINTS

● When you lay out the cord in step one, be sure that the top of the middle loop is the exact center of the cord, or your cord ends will not be the same length after tightening. When you take the slack out, start from the same point.

《 TYING PROCESS 》

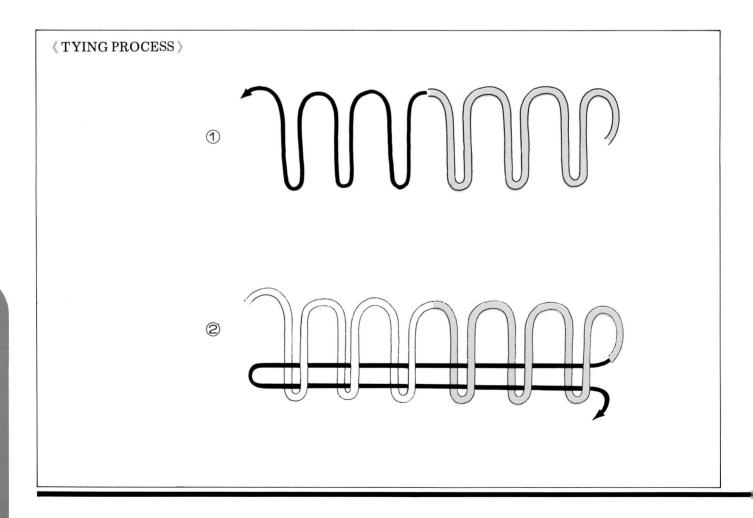

③

④ Use both ends to do the weaving, so that they meet in the center.

⑤

⑥ completed knot

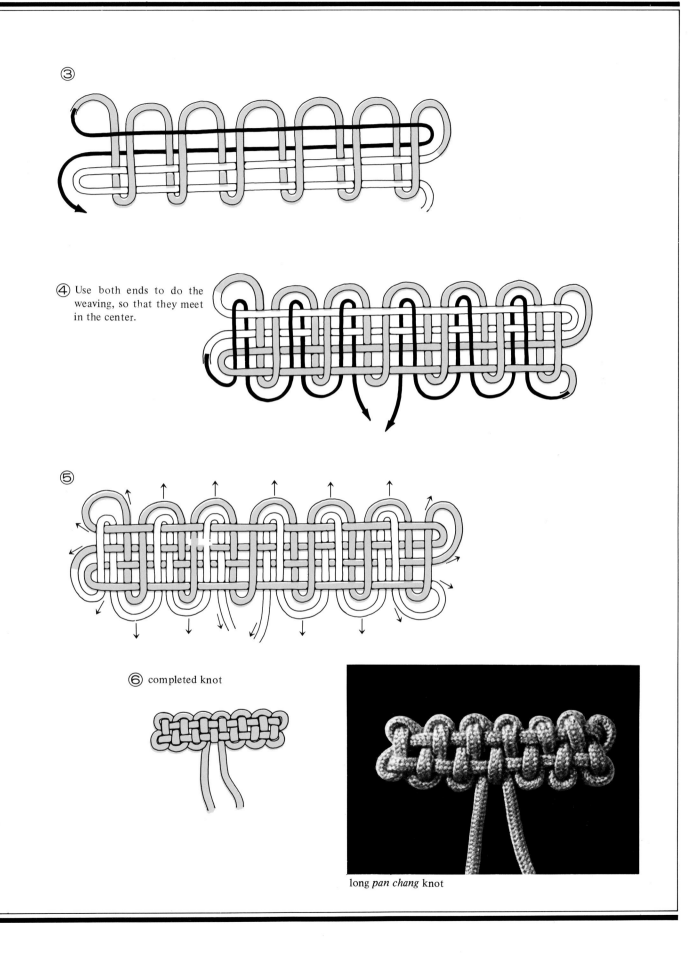

long *pan chang* knot

STONE CHIME KNOT

The stone chime is an ancient Chinese percussion instrument made with an L-shaped piece of sonorous stone or jade. A series of them, graduated according to size and thickness, is often hung from a two-tiered wooden rack. Used in ritual orchestral ensembles, the appropriate stone chime when called for is struck with a mallet, its crisp tone marking the end of a musical phrase. Stone chimes are indispensable in Confucian music, which is noted for its grandeur and symbolism. Musical performance in this tradition is an expression of social ethics. The music of the sage-ruler deeply moves his listeners, the people, steering them toward righteousness, and creating lasting peace under the heavens.

TYING

The stone chime knot is made up of two long *pan chang* knots woven together at right angles, sharing a common corner. The warp and woof of each *pan chang* can be increased to make a larger stone chime knot. The weaving pattern is the same as in any *pan chang* or variation.

HINTS

● The only problem you'll have with this knot is the tightening. Tighten one long *pan chang* completely first. Then watch out for distortion in the common corner when you tighten the other one.

《TYING PROCESS》

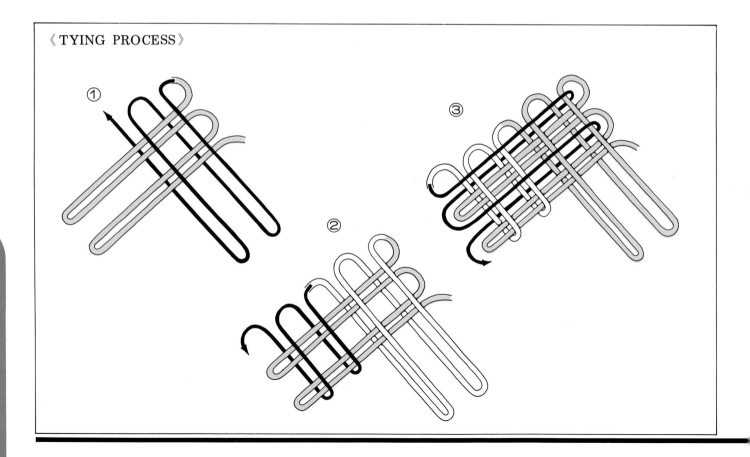

① ② ③

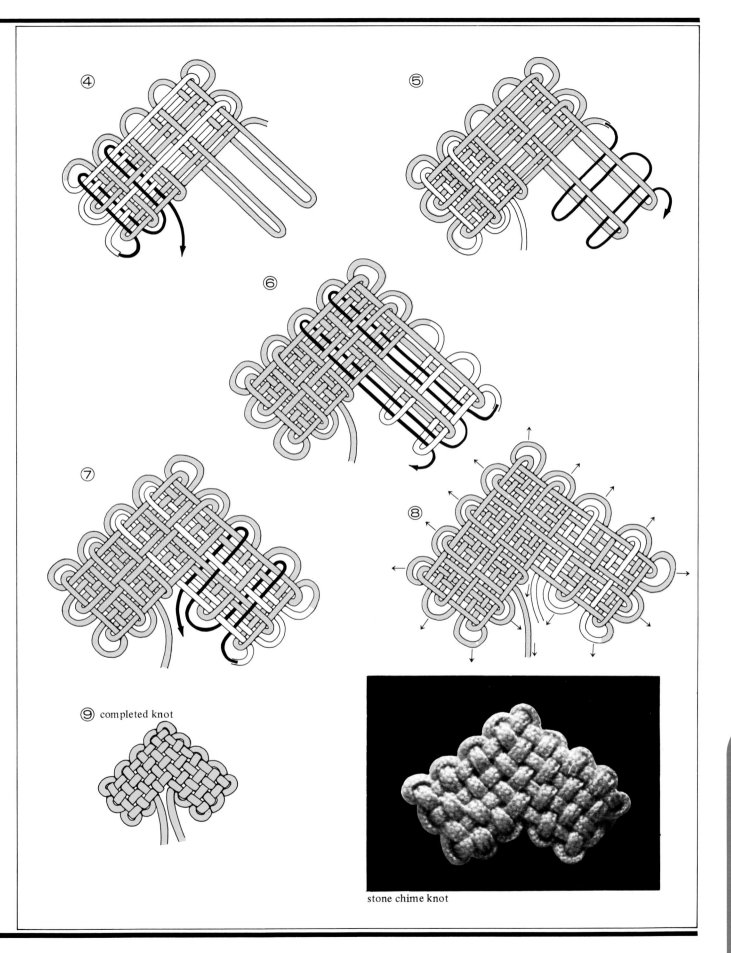

④

⑤

⑥

⑦

⑧

⑨ completed knot

stone chime knot

DOUBLE DIAMOND KNOT

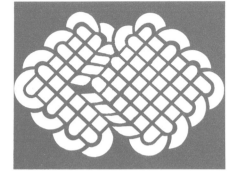

方勝

The double diamond, a woman's traditional hair ornament, has been used in China for centuries. The famous drama *The West Chamber*, by Wang Shih-fu of the Yuan Dynasty, contains a passage that describes how they were made at that time. According to that reference, a double diamond hair ornament is born from two pieces of square embroidery woven together in its characteristic shape. Knotted varieties were also popular, the more colorful of which were made with red or peach-colored cord. Elegance called for a double diamond hair ornament worked with patterns in gold and silver thread. They were often dangled from the hairpins gracing the center of gathered hairstyles, providing a convenient place to hang a tiny piece of prized jade or a favorite embroidered sachet.

TYING

The double diamond knot is simple to do, though it requires a lot of patience. First tie a stone chime knot and tighten it. Then tie a large *pan chang*, linking the outer loops that are adjacent to the stone chime knot through the outer loops of that knot, so that the two knots form a single unit.

HINTS

● Use a long cord, and when you tighten the stone chime knot, make sure that you start from the top and tighten in both directions. If you end up with two loose ends of different lengths, it may be impossible to complete the *pan chang.*
● To make the seam even, make sure that the four links between the two knots all go through in the same direction.

《 TYING PROCESS 》

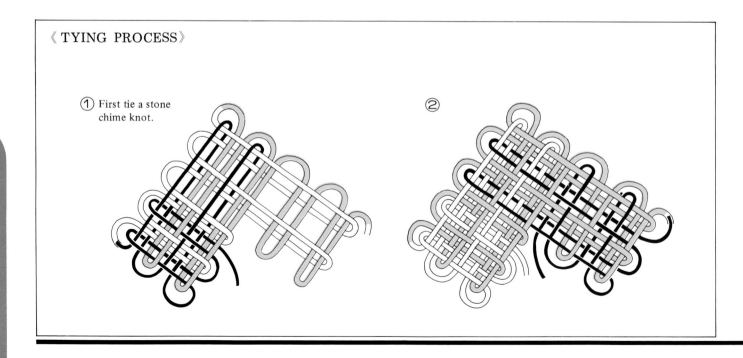

① First tie a stone chime knot.

②

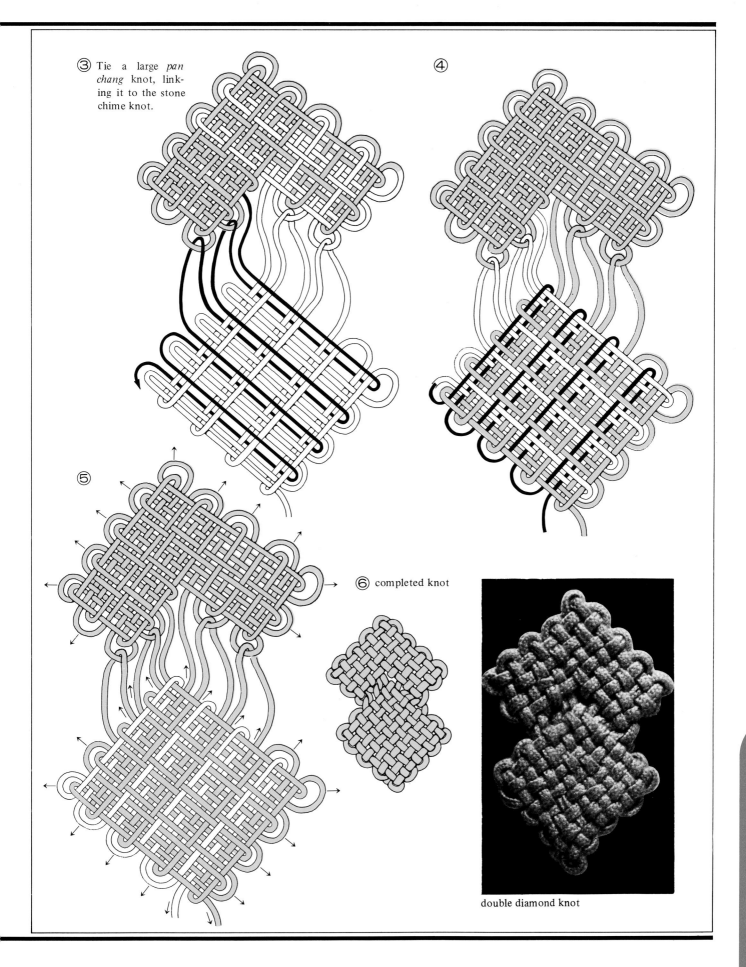

③ Tie a large *pan chang* knot, linking it to the stone chime knot.

④

⑤

⑥ completed knot

double diamond knot

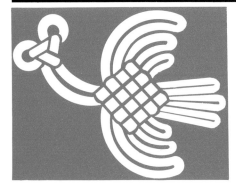

仙鶴

CRANE KNOT

The crane is an often-employed symbol of longevity. Quite naturally, it is the favored pet of the God of Longevity, and is often seen in his company. A little less naturally, but quite poetically, it embodies the aspirations of many a Taoist sage. Those virtuous enough to achieve immortality undergo transformation — sprouting wings, growing feathers, and becoming cranes. Once their souls are unfettered as cranes, they soar into the sky, glancing at the world of bondage far below, delighting in a freedom unimagined by the pedestrian and worry-ridden mortal.

TYING

Tying the crane knot is extremely simple. The head is a two-loop cloverleaf knot, coming down to form a *pan chang* for the body. The neck, wings, and tail are all sewn together after the knot has been tightened.

HINTS

● If you use a stiff cord, it will prevent the wings and tail from drooping.
● Pay attention to the lengths of the loops that will make up the wings.
● After the tail is completed, you can hide the loose ends in the *pan chang* knot.

《TYING PROCESS》

① First tie a two-loop cloverleaf knot.

②

③

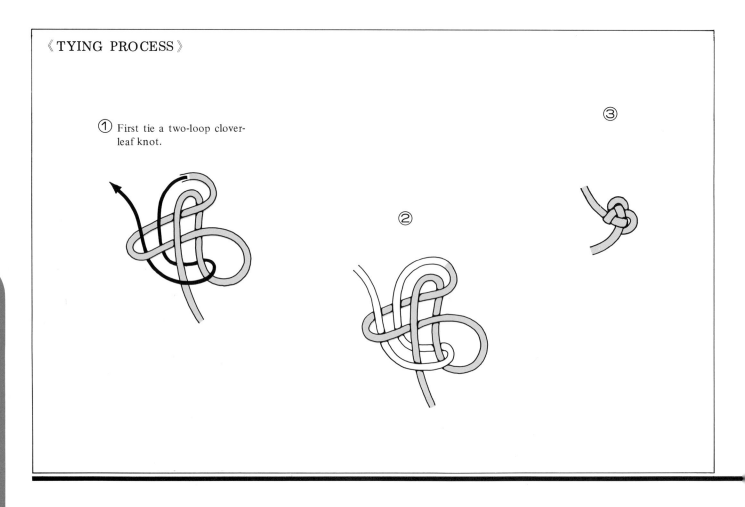

④ Tie a *pan chang* knot to form the body.

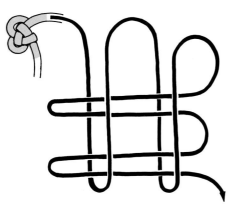

⑤

⑥

⑦ Leave the loops closest to the head long, and those closest to the tail short, to form the wings.

⑧ Hide one of the cord ends in the *pan chang* knot. Use the other to form the tail feathers, then hide it in the *pan chang,* too. Stitch the neck, wings, and tail in place.

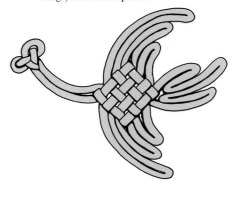

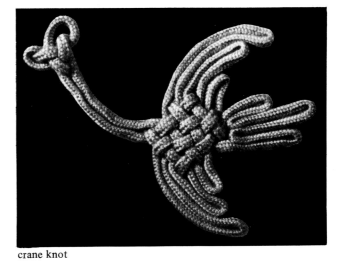

crane knot

PHOENIX KNOT

According to the *Classic of the Mountains and Seas,* the first pair of phoenix were born somewhere near the southern extremity of the world, in a mountain valley that faces the sun. Thus the phoenix has come to symbolize, among a host of other things, the sun and warmth, and it presides over the southern quadrant. The phoenix is the king of birds and the essence of the supernatural. It will nest only in the *wu tung* tree, and will eat nothing but the seeds of the finest bamboo. It drinks only from the sweetest of springs. When it takes to the air, all the birds in the sky follow at its tail. Occasionally, it shows itself among humans, demonstrating by its mere presence that all will be peaceful and right in the world. Together with the tortoise, dragon, and unicorn, the phoenix holds a post in the quadrumvirate of Chinese super-supernaturals.

TYING

The head of the phoenix is made up of a cloverleaf knot and a small *pan chang.* A larger *pan chang* makes up the body. Again, the only difficult thing is the sewing. The leftover loops and loose ends are sewn into head plumes, wings, tail feathers, etc., as shown. The two neck feathers and the last two tail feathers are sewn with separate pieces of cord linked through their respective *pan chang* knots.

HINTS

● Make the *pan chang* in the head tighter vertically than horizontally, so that it will be oblong in shape.
● After you form the first four loops of the tail, pass the cord ends back through the corner of the *pan chang* to anchor them into position.

《TYING PROCESS》

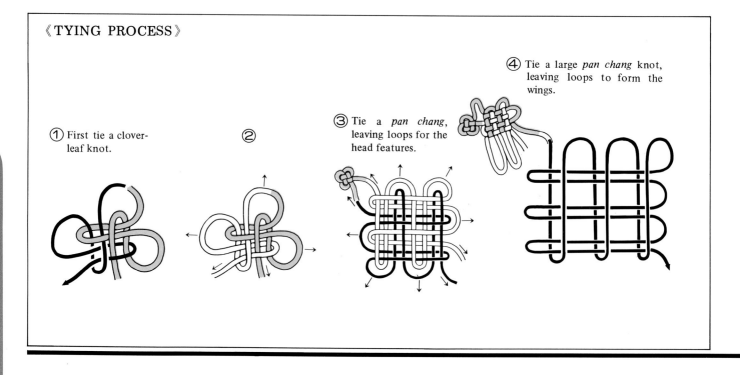

① First tie a cloverleaf knot.

②

③ Tie a *pan chang,* leaving loops for the head features.

④ Tie a large *pan chang* knot, leaving loops to form the wings.

⑤

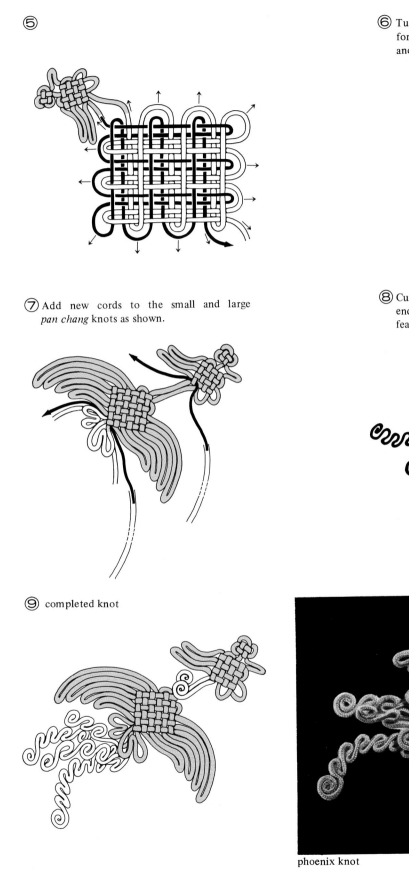

⑥ Turn the knot 90°. Use the loose ends to form tail feathers. Shape the head features and stitch them in place.

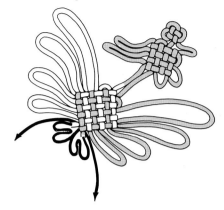

⑦ Add new cords to the small and large *pan chang* knots as shown.

⑧ Curl the new cords and the original cord ends into additional feathers. Stitch the feathers, wings, and head features in place.

⑨ completed knot

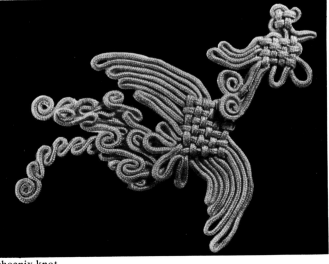

phoenix knot

TEN-ACCORD KNOT

The ten-accord knot symbolizes all of the things that make up the good life in Chinese eyes. They include: manifold returns from a single investment, two hearts living together in harmony, passing all three levels of civil examinations with flying colors, peace throughout the four seasons, a bountiful harvest of all five major grains, the vigor of spring growth in all six Chinese cardinal directions, being blessed with seven successful sons, a life longer than any of the eight immortals, nine generations under one roof, and complete prosperity and wealth.

TYING

The ten-accord is similar to the brocade ball knot, but instead of five cloverleaf knots, you are using five double coin knots.

HINTS

● Don't tighten the knots too much, or the final product will not have a regular round shape.
● You will have to stitch the ten-accord knot together for it to retain its shape.

《TYING PROCESS》

① First tie a double coin knot.

②

③

④ Cross the two cord ends, and use each one to tie another double coin knot, linking each with the first double coin knot.

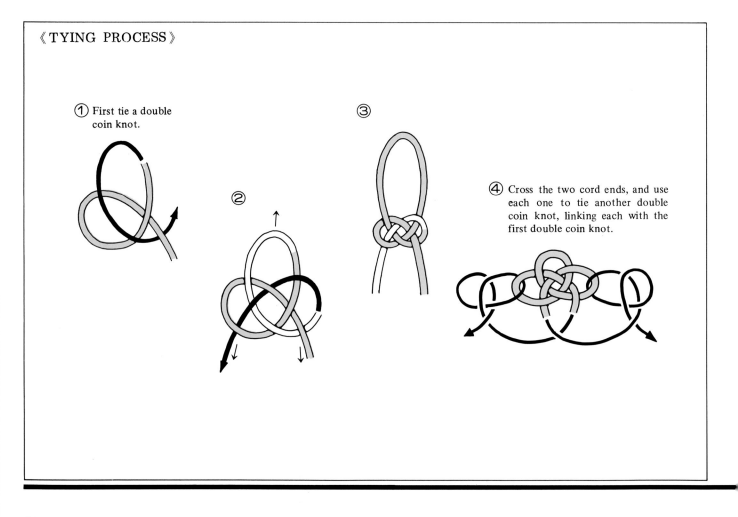

⑤

⑥ Weave the cord ends through the cord segments that connect the three knots to form another double coin knot.

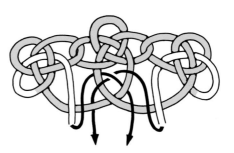

⑦ Cross the two ends and use them to tie a final double coin knot, linking it to the two side ones.

⑧

⑨ completed knot

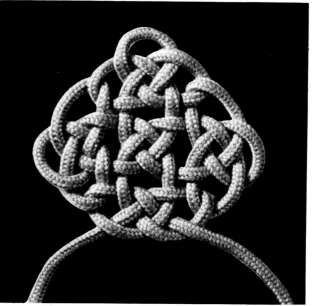

ten-accord knot

CREATIVE APPLICATIONS

Although decorative Chinese knotting comes from a tradition of days gone by, it need not be studied merely for its quaintness or antiquity. The ancient motifs can be used to ornament the everyday objects of our present lives, lending a touch of rare personalized beauty and "Chineseness" to virtually any object.

The following pages contain instructions, drawings, and photographs for 41 such practical creative applications. If you have mastered the basic and compound knots, you shouldn't have any trouble tying them. The individual knots in each composition are numbered in order of completion. The only problem might be cord length. Study how many knots are to be tied with any given cord, and make sure you use enough to allow you to work them all in.

Among these creative applications are necklaces from which to hang pendants, necklaces with knotted pendants of their own, knotted belts, and wrap-around belts with decorative knotwork at the ends reminiscent of Chinese sashes of old. There are intricate buttons that can be attached to clothing and purses. Examples are given of how to add sparkle to embroidery with the use of knotting, and there are grand combinations that can be used independently as wall hangings.

Of course, these 41 combinations by no means represent all of the possibilities. They are just meant to give you an idea of the infinite number of ways the knots can be put together and used. Having come this far, there's no reason why you can't blend the old Chinese tradition with your own artistic imagination to create masterpieces of your own.

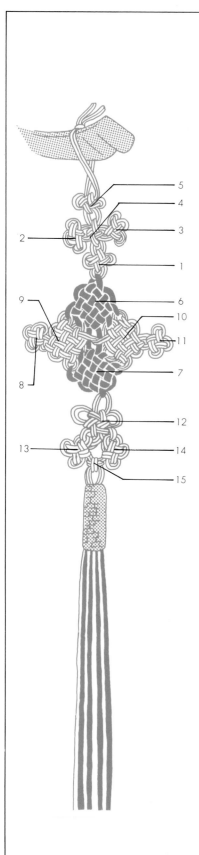

1

This knot combination is tied with four separate cords. Begin with the five cloverleaf knots at the top. Tie them from the bottom up, in the order shown. This is actually a *ju i* knot with an additional cloverleaf tied below it. Pass a new cord through the bottom loop of the lowest cloverleaf knot in the completed portion. Tie two *pan chang* knots with this cord, top to bottom, knots 6 and 7. Hide the loose ends in the body of the last *pan chang*. Using another cord, tie a cloverleaf, knot 8, and follow it with a *pan chang*, knot 9. While tying this *pan chang*, link each outer loop to those on the adjacent sides of the *pan chang* knots above and below it. After knot 9 is completed, pass the ends through the loop between the top and bottom *pan chang* knots, and begin another *pan chang*, knot 10, on the right. Remember to link all the side loops into the *pan chang* knots above and below. At the end of this *pan chang*, hide one loose end back in the body of the knot. Use the other loose end to tie a cloverleaf knot, and then hide this end in the *pan chang*, too. Pass a new cord through the bottom loop of the entire configuration. Tie a round brocade knot with five complete loops, knot 12. Use the loose end on the left to tie a cloverleaf knot, linking its first loop with the bottom left loop of the round brocade knot. Then use the loose end on the right to repeat the process. Bring the two loose ends, one from each cloverleaf, together to tie a cross knot. Finish the piece off with tassels attached to the loose ends, if desired.

2

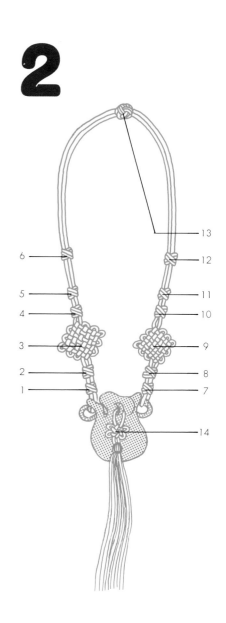

This necklace is made of two separate knotted sections, each starting at an edge of the pendant and working up. The two sides are tied in the same pattern. Begin with the left side, passing the cord through the handle of the small ceramic pendant. Then, as in the numbered sequence, tie two double connection knots, a large *pan chang* knot, and three more double connection knots. Repeat the process on the right side. Then, using the two loose ends on the right as if they were a single cord end, and the two on the left as another cord end, tie a double-cord button knot. Hide all four loose ends in its center. Pass another cord through the eyelet on the front of the pendant and use it to tie a six-loop round brocade knot, adding tassels to the bottom loop if desired.

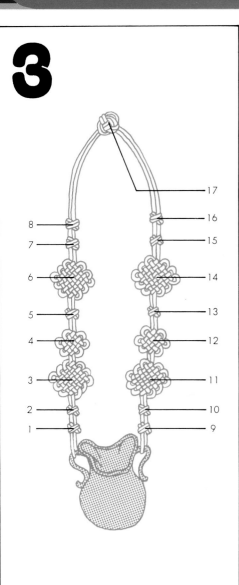

This necklace is made in the same way as the necklace in creative application 2, except that a different sequence of knots is used. Work from the bottom up, tying two double connection knots, a large *pan chang* knot, a standard *pan chang* knot, another double connection knot, another large *pan chang* knot, and two more double connection knots. Once again, the final button knot uses all four cord ends.

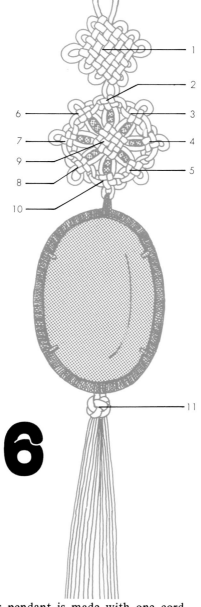

4

Begin this simple necklace with a standard button knot. Use one free end to tie a series of flat button knots. After you have reached the desired length, loop the loose end back on itself and wrap it with thread or wire. Hide the unused end from the first button knot in the same manner. To stabilize the necklace, run a thin piece of wire around the back of the flat button knots, stitching it to the center of each knot. Hang the pendant off the center of the wire.

5

This pendant is tied with two cords. Tie a *pan chang* knot with the first cord, and leave the ends free. Use a second cord to tie a round brocade knot with five loops. Pass the ends of the first cord through the back of the round brocade knot, bringing them out parallel to the cords that emerge from this knot. Begin another round brocade knot with both of these cords together. This knot is the center of the pendant, and will have a total of six outer loops. As it is being tied, the two cords separate when they reach an outer loop. The first cord is pulled close to the body of the center round brocade knot when it reaches an outer loop. The second cord, on the other hand, is used to tie a five-loop round brocade knot into each outer loop of the central double-cord knot. As each one of these outer round brocade knots is tied, the first loop on the left hooks into the adjacent loop of the outer round brocade knot above it. The six outer loops of the center knot,

and the smaller round brocade knots on them, are tied in the sequence numbered in the diagram. When all six are done, the center knot is completed. The two loose ends of the first cord are hidden in the body of the center knot. The other two loose ends are tied into another five-loop round brocade knot, linking into the ones on the right and left. Hide one of the loose ends in the body of this knot. String the pendant onto the other loose end, and then hide that one too.

6

This pendant is made with one cord. Begin by tying a *pan chang* knot. Beneath this, add a cloverleaf knot. Then start a small *pan chang* knot with the loose ends. While you are tying this *pan chang*, add a cloverleaf knot on every outer loop. Link the adjacent loops of the outer ring of cloverleaf knots together. When you finish knot 8, the completion of the center *pan chang* follows. Once this is done, tie another cloverleaf knot below it with the two loose ends. Add the pendant to the bottom loop of this cloverleaf. Hide the loose ends in the body of the knot. The little beads are stitched into place after the entire knot is tied. The button knot at the bottom of the pendant is tied separately, and the top ends of the tassels are hidden within it.

4

5

6

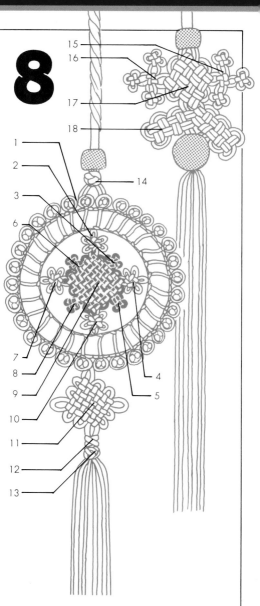

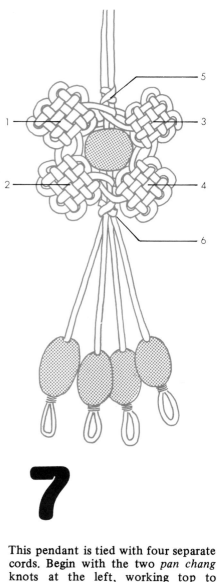

This wrap-around belt is made in three stages. The two pieces of knotwork at the ends of the belt are done first, and then they are attached to the thick cord that makes up the wrap-around portion of the belt. The ring used as the base for the knotwork on one end of the belt is jade, but a ring of any material will serve the purpose. Once you have selected your ring, enclose it with lock stitches, using the cord that will be tied onto the outside of the ring. When you finish the stitches, tie a simple knot so they will not come undone. Use another piece of the same cord to tie a continuous series of two-loop cloverleaf knots around the outer edge of the ring. Each two-loop cloverleaf knot uses the outside portion of a lock stitch as one loop of the knot. After the outside of the ring has been encircled, hide the loose end of the cord in the stitching. The knot in the center of the ring is tied next. Use one cord to tie a round brocade knot with five complete loops. Add a second cord to the loose ends, and use all four to tie a large *pan chang* below the round brocade knot. As you tie the *pan chang*, use the second cord to add a cloverleaf knot on each of the center loops of the four sides of the *pan chang*. When you reach the corners of the *pan chang*, use the first cord to tie a round brocade knot on those loops before continuing back into the body of the *pan chang*. These outer knots will be completed in the sequence numbered in the diagram. After knot 8 is tied, the completion of the *pan chang* follows. Once it is done, use the first cord to tie a five-loop round brocade knot below it. Hide the loose ends in the body of the round brocade knot. The loose ends of the second cord are hidden directly in the body of the *pan chang* knot. Sew this completed piece of knotwork into the ring, attaching it at the extremities of all four round brocade knots. Pass another cord through the bottom of the outer edge of the ring. Use it to tie a *pan chang*, followed by a double connection knot and a button knot. Pass two cords through the top of the outer edge of the ring, and use them to tie a button knot. Leave the ends free to attach them to the thick cord that makes up the wrap-around portion of the belt. Then do the knotwork that will be attached to the other end. Begin with two cords, tying them as if they were one, and leaving extra cord at the top for later attaching. Use the double cord to tie a *pan chang*. As you

tie it, tie a *ju i* knot into both the left and right corner loops. Each *ju i* is tied with only one of the cords. The other is drawn close to the body of the *pan chang*. Once the *pan chang* is complete, tie a small stone chime knot below it. String a bead onto the leftover cord ends, adding tassels if you desire. The connection between the loose ends and the tassels can be hidden within the bead. Adding the wrap-around portion of the belt is the same for both ends. First string a large bead onto each end of the thick belt cord you have chosen. Then wrap the ends of the thick belt cord onto the cords coming out of the top of each piece of knotwork — the loose ends from the button knot on one end, and the large top loop from the *pan chang* on the other end. Make these connections as close to the actual knotting as possible, so that the thread used to do the wrapping can be hidden in the large beads.

7

This pendant is tied with four separate cords. Begin with the two *pan chang* knots at the left, working top to bottom. Be sure to leave a large loop at the right corner of each *pan chang* to accommodate the center cord later on. Hide the loose ends in the body of the last *pan chang*. With a new cord, tie the two *pan chang* knots on the right, linking them to the ones on the left at the adjacent corners with identically large loops. Hide the ends. Use yet another cord to tie a double connection knot. Then pass this cord through the loops that hook the two top *pan chang* knots together. String a bead onto the cord and pass the cord through the loops that hook the bottom *pan chang* knots together. Tie a double connection knot to hold everything in place. Add another cord and sew it on inside the double connection knot, and string beads on the four cord ends if desired. Loop each cord end back on itself and wrap it with thread or wire.

7

8

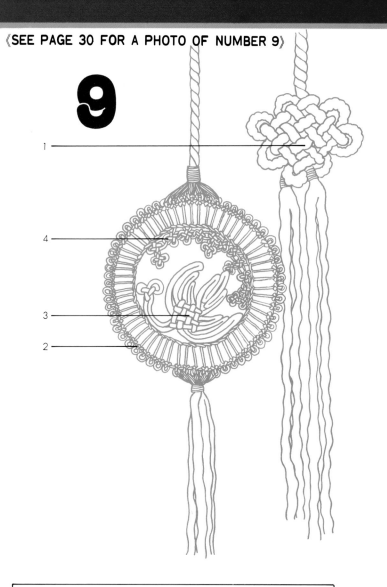

9

The body of this wrap-around belt is a long thick cord. Tie a *pan chang* knot at one end of the thick cord. Hide one of the loose ends in the body of the knot. The other end is left free to make up the wrap-around portion of the belt. Stitch the *pan chang* in place, and hook an additional cord through its bottom loop to serve as a tassel, binding the connection with thread. The knotting at the other end of the belt can be done separately and attached to the wrap-around cord after it is completed. Select a ring for the base. The one pictured is jade, but any material will do. First, enclose the ring with lock stitches, using the same cord that you will use on the outside of the ring. Tie off the end of the stitching to hold it in place and hide the loose ends in it. Use another piece of the same cord to tie a continuous series of two-loop cloverleaf knots around the outer edge of the ring. The corresponding loop from the lock stitching acts as one loop for each of these two-loop cloverleaf knots. Once the circle is complete, hide the loose end of the knotting in the lock stitching. Use another cord to tie a crane knot. With yet another cord, tie a group of cloverleaf knots in a configuration that will provide a balance for the crane knot. Sew these two pieces of knotwork into the inner edge of the ring, stitched onto the lock stitches. To attach the completed ring to the belt, unravel the end of the thick wrap-around cord a bit. Pass the unraveled ends through the loops of the two-loop cloverleaf knots at the top of the ring. Bring these ends back up to the unraveled portion of the thick cord and wrap them in place with thread. The tassels at the bottom of the ring are made of unraveled thick cord, and are attached in the same way.

10

This belt is made in much the same way as the belt in creative application 11. Start from the center knot, a very large *pan chang*. Continue to the left, adding a *ju i* with its large end facing away from the center, a *pan chang* slightly smaller than the center one, a *ju i* with its large end facing the preceding *pan chang*, and a small *pan chang*. A series of double connection knots finishes this side of the belt. When you have reached the desired length, make a loop with one of the cord ends before sewing it and the other cord end in place and hiding them in the body of the last double connection knot. Hook a new cord into the right-hand corner loop of the center *pan chang*, and repeat the series of knots, knots 7 through 11, on the right. Finish this side off with a button knot, and hide the loose ends in its center.

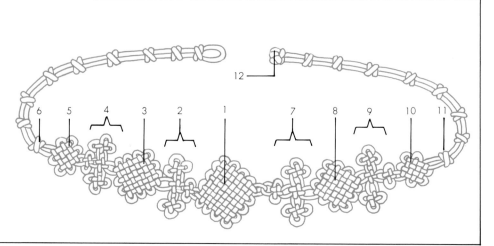

11

This belt is tied in two sections. The series of knots to the left and right of the center knotwork are exactly the same. Begin with the knotwork in the center. First, tie a *ju i* knot. Follow it with a large *pan chang* that has a *ju i* tied into each corner loop. Add another *ju i* at the end of the *pan chang*, with its large end facing the *pan chang*. Continue with the same cord, working to the left. In succession, tie a large *pan chang* with a cloverleaf knot in the top and bottom corner loops, a *ju i* with its large end facing away from the *pan chang*, a small *pan chang*, another *ju i*, a small *pan chang*, and enough double coin knots to complete the belt. When you have reached the desired length, tie a double connection knot. Make a loop with one cord end and sew it and the other cord end in the body of the double connection knot. Now, turn to the right-hand side of the belt. Hook a new cord through the extreme right-hand loop of the center knotwork, and repeat the series, knots 15 through 22. When you have finished the double coin knots on this side, tie a button knot and hide the loose ends in the center of it.

11

10

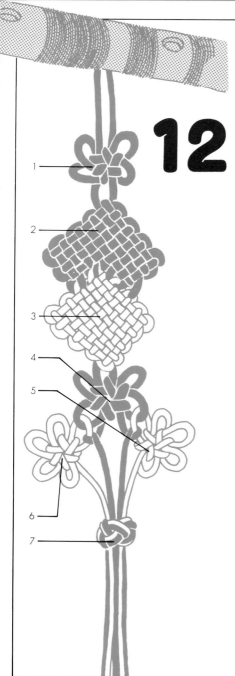

12

This ornament is pictured attached to a Chinese flute, but it can be hung almost anywhere. The knotwork is done with four separate cords. Begin with the first cord, using it to tie a round brocade knot with five complete loops. Below this, tie a stone chime knot with the same cord, forming the first half of a double diamond knot. Leave the free ends hanging loose. Use another cord to tie a *pan chang* knot below the stone chime knot, hooking it into the stone chime knot to form the second half of a double diamond knot. When the *pan chang* is done, hide the loose ends in its body. Weave the loose ends from the center of the stone chime knot through the center of the *pan chang* to come out at the bottom. There, use this cord to tie a round brocade knot, knot 4, with five complete loops. Leave the loose ends hanging for the time being. Use another cord to tie a five-loop round brocade knot, knot 6, linking it to the lower left loop of knot 4. Hide one of the loose ends in the body of the knot, and leave the other one free. Use yet another cord to repeat the process on the right, hooking a five-loop round brocade knot into the lower right loop of knot 4, and hiding one of the cord ends in the body of the knot. Then loop the cord ends hanging from knot 4 through the respective linked loops of knots 5 and 6. Use the end on the left along with the remaining cord from knot 6 as a single cord end, and the end on the right along with the remaining cord end from knot 5 as another cord end, to tie a double-cord button knot. Leave extra cord dangling for tassels, if desired.

14

This is an example of knotting used with traditional Chinese chops. Thread a cord through the center hole of the chop, and tie a double connection knot to secure it. Finish with a good luck knot.

15

This decoration is seen adorning the handle of a fan in the picture. It is tied with two cords as if they were one. After hooking the cords through the eyelet of the object to be adorned, tie a button knot and a butterfly knot below it. Below these, begin a good luck knot. When you reach the left and right outer loops of the good luck knot, tie a double-cord double coin knot into each of them. Finish the good luck knot, and leave the loose ends dangling as tassels.

13

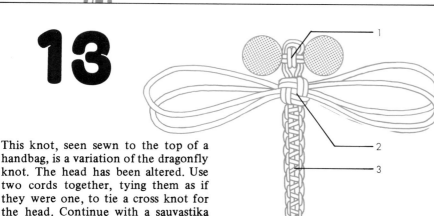

This knot, seen sewn to the top of a handbag, is a variation of the dragonfly knot. The head has been altered. Use two cords together, tying them as if they were one, to tie a cross knot for the head. Continue with a sauvastika knot, and then a series of flat knots. The eyes are large beads sewn on after the knotting is completed.

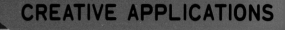

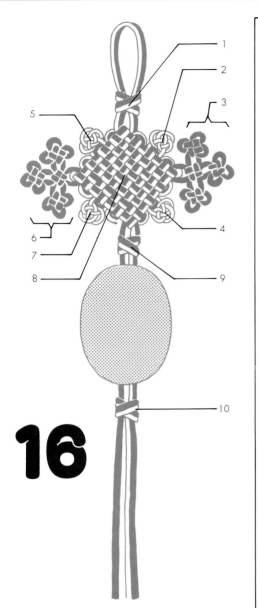

16

This ornament, shown decorating the ends of a Chinese scroll painting in the picture, can be used almost anywhere. The knotting is done with two cords tied as if they were one. Use the double cord to tie a double connection knot. Below this, begin a large *pan chang* knot. As the *pan chang* is being tied, one of the cords is used to tie a double coin knot into each of the outer loops in the center of the sides. The other cord is used to tie a *ju i* knot into the loops at the left and right corners. These knots are tied in the sequence numbered in the diagram, and after knot 7 is finished, the completion of the *pan chang* follows. Below that, tie a double-cord double connection knot. String the pendant on, then tie another double connection knot to secure it. Leave extra cord as tassels, if desired.

This ornament is seen hanging from a lampshade in the picture, but it can be hung almost anywhere. Use one cord to tie a balanced good luck knot and a button knot below it. Then tie a round brocade knot with five outer loops. Add a second cord to the two loose ends, and tie another round brocade knot with the double cord. In the outer loops of this central round brocade knot, the second cord is pulled tight against the body of the knot. The first cord, on the other hand, goes on to tie a round brocade knot into each outer loop of the central knot. These knots are tied in the sequence numbered in the diagram, and are linked together through their adjacent loops. After knot 7 is finished, the central knot is completed. The loose ends of the second cord can be hidden in the body of the knot. Use the loose ends from the first cord to tie another round brocade knot to complete the circle. Add another cord to the loose ends, and tie a double-cord button knot. Leave extra cord dangling for tassels, if desired.

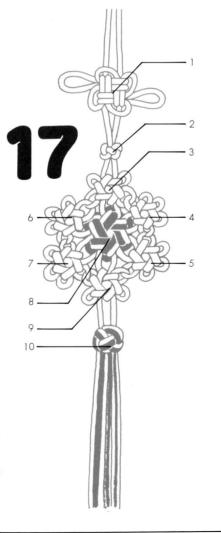

17

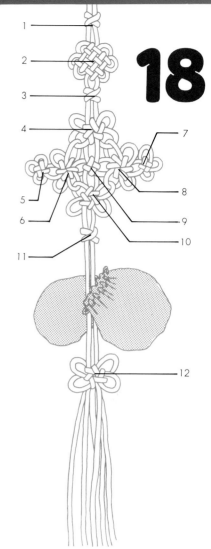

18

This knot combination is seen on the end of a wrap-around belt in the picture. Begin by tying a double connection knot, a *pan chang*, and another double connection knot below it. Then tie a round brocade knot with five loops. Use the left cord end only to tie another round brocade knot, linking it to the first round brocade knot at their adjacent loops, and tying a cloverleaf knot into its extreme left loop before finishing it. Use the right cord end to repeat the process on the right side. Then use the two free cord ends and the sections of cord between knots 4 and 6 and knots 4 and 8 to tie a cloverleaf knot in the center. This is just like tying the center cloverleaf in a *ju i* knot. Below this, tie another round brocade knot using both loose ends, linking it with the adjacent loops of the round brocade knots on the sides. Tie a double connection knot, attach the pouches, and then tie another round brocade knot at the bottom. Leave the ends dangling as tassels. To make a fuller tassel, pass additional cords through the body of the round brocade knot and leave them dangling.

《SEE PAGES 20-21 FOR PHOTOS OF THESE KNOTS》

19

20

21

22

This decoration is tied from the bottom up. Start with a round brocade knot with four loops, linking the bottom two to the pendant. Then use the left cord end to begin a cloverleaf knot. As you are tying this knot, link it to the round brocade knot by means of their adjacent loops, and tie an additional cloverleaf knot, knot 2, into its left loop. Then finish the last loop in knot 3. With the free end, tie another cloverleaf knot above these two, linking it with the adjacent loop of knot 3. Then use the loose cord end on the right to repeat the entire process on that side. Bring the two loose ends together and tie yet another cloverleaf knot, again linking the side loops into the adjacent loops of the previously tied knots. Tie a double connection knot to close off the piece. The bead in the center is sewn on after the knotting is completed.

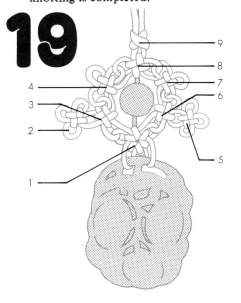

The center knot in this composition is an example of what you can do with two different colored cords tied into one knot. To begin, use one cord to tie the round brocade knot at the top. String a bead onto the loose ends, and sew another cord of a different color to them. Then use this double cord to tie a stone chime knot. Make sure that the cords lie side by side throughout the entire stone chime knot — don't allow them to cross over one another at any point. Hide the loose ends in the body of the knot. The two pendants are sewn on after the knot is completed.

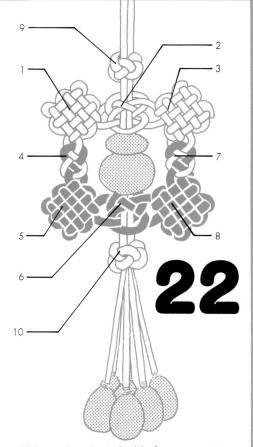

This pendant is tied with three separate cords. Use one to tie the upper half of the square frame. Working from left to right, tie a *pan chang* knot, leaving extra cord in the bottom corner loop. Next to this, tie a rather loose double coin knot, and another *pan chang*, again leaving extra cord in the bottom loop. Hide the two loose ends in the body of the last *pan chang*. With another cord, tie the bottom half of the square, again working left to right. Tie another *pan chang*, knot 5, but when you reach the upper corner loop, tie the cord into the extra cord you left at the bottom of knot 1 to form a double coin knot, knot 4. When the *pan chang* is finished, tie a double coin knot to the right, and add another *pan chang*, again connecting it to the *pan chang* above it by means of a double coin knot in the corner loop. Hide the loose ends in the body of the *pan chang*. The third cord passes vertically through the center of the pendant. First, tie a button knot on this cord. Then pass the loose ends through the double coin knot that connects the top two *pan chang* knots. String the beads onto the cord ends, and pass the ends through the double coin knot that connects the bottom two *pan chang* knots. Tie a button knot below the entire configuration. Add extra cord and beads for tassels, if desired, hiding the loose ends in the body of the button knot.

The center of this framed hanging is a piece of embroidery. The twelve knots around it, each tied separately, are sewn directly onto the background cloth. Six of them are longevity knots with the bottom loops closed and the loose ends hidden in the bodies of the knots. The other six knots are each tied with two cords. Use one cord to tie a six-loop round brocade knot, hiding the loose ends in the body. Pass another cord through one of the loops, and start a stone chime knot. At the center loop of each short edge of the stone chime knot, tie a *ju i* knot. After the stone chime is completed, add three double connection knots and a *pan chang* knot, hiding the loose ends in the body of the *pan chang*. When all the knots are done, stitch them on to the background cloth.

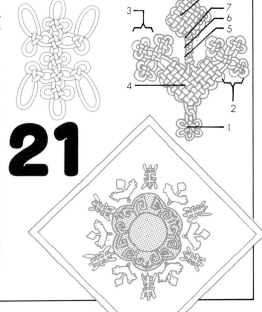

23

24

25

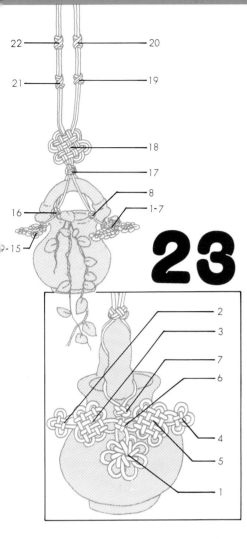

23

This creation is shown in two photos — a full view and a close-up side view of the knotwork on each handle of the small ceramic pot. It is at the handle that the knotting begins. First, use one cord to tie a round brocade knot with seven loops. Use the left cord end to tie a *pan chang* knot, adding a cloverleaf knot in the far corner loop. Repeat the pattern with the right cord end from the round brocade knot. Then use the two cord ends and the sections of cord connecting the *pan chang* knots and the round brocade knot to tie a cloverleaf knot, just like tying the center cloverleaf in a *ju i* knot. Add a button knot, and pass the loose ends around the handle in opposite directions to tie another button knot on the inside of the handle. Use another cord to tie this entire configuration over again on the other end of the handle. Then bring all four loose ends together at the very top of the handle, and tie a double-cord button knot to hold the handle decorations tight. Continue using the double cords to tie a *pan chang* knot, then separate the pairs of cords and use each to tie a series of double connection knots.

24 ➤

Two cords are used to tie this piece of knotwork. Begin on the left handle. Use one cord to tie a *ju i* knot, and pass the loose ends through the handle in opposite directions. Then tie a button knot directly above the handle. Use another cord to repeat the process on the right handle. This will leave a total of four loose cord ends to work with. Take the innermost two, and bring them together in the center of the pendant to tie a button knot and a large *pan chang* above it. Then return to the left handle, and use the remaining free cord end to tie a cloverleaf knot above the button knot on that side. Pass the end through the left corner loop of the completed *pan chang* knot. Repeat the process with the loose cord end on the right handle. Bring both loose ends up to the loose ends from the *pan chang* knot, and use all four cords to tie a double connection knot above it.

◄

This composition is tied with a single cord. Tie a stone chime knot, linking the bottom corner loops through the handles of the pendant. Weave the two loose ends of the completed stone chime knot back through the body of the knot so that they come out directly above it. There, tie a double connection knot, a round brocade knot with ten loops, and another double connection knot.

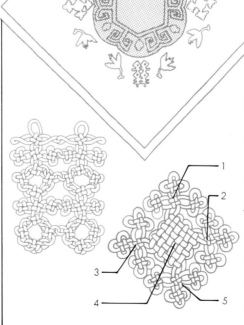

25

The center of this framed hanging is a piece of embroidery. The twelve knots around it are sewn directly onto the background cloth. Each is tied separately. Eight of them are merely individual crane knots. The knots at the top and bottom are individual double happiness knots. Each of the other two is tied with a single cord, beginning with a *ju i* knot. Beneath the *ju i* knot, begin a large *pan chang* knot, tying an additional *ju i* knot into both the left and right corner loops. When the *pan chang* knot is done, use the cord ends to tie a final *ju i* at the bottom corner. Hide the loose ends in the body of the knot. Once all the knots are tied, stitch them into place on the background cloth.

26

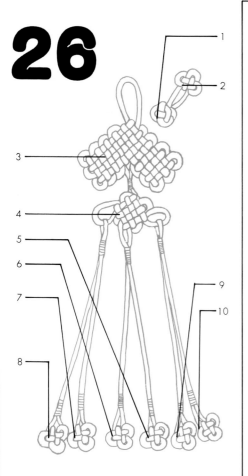

This fastener is tied with two separate sets of knots. The button part is a button knot and a cloverleaf knot, with the cord ends hidden in the body of the cloverleaf. With another cord, tie a stone chime knot to begin the lower part. Leave enough space in the top loop to allow the button knot to pass through it. When the stone chime knot is finished, use thread to bind a segment of the loose cord ends together. Then tie a *pan chang* knot with large loops on the left and right corners. Again, bind a segment of the loose ends together, and let them hang down. Tie each off in a cloverleaf knot, and bring each cord end back up to bind it in place just above each cloverleaf knot. Then pass one new cord each through the left and right corner loops of the *pan chang* knot. Bind them just below the links to hold them in place, tie all four loose ends off in cloverleaf knots, and bind them like the other two loose ends.

The top part of this fastener is made up of four cloverleaf knots. Begin with the one at the bottom. Use the free cord end on the left to tie another one, linking its lower side loop into the adjacent loop of the first knot. Do the same with the right cord end. Then bring the two cord ends together to tie the last cloverleaf knot, linking both of its side loops into the adjacent loops of the knots on its sides. The button is sewn onto the bottom knot. Using a new cord, tie a plafond knot to begin the bottom section, leaving enough space in the top loop to accommodate the button. Tie a cloverleaf knot below the plafond knot. Then use the left cord end and the left loop of the cloverleaf to tie another cloverleaf knot, knot 7. The free cord end will emerge from this knot pointing back toward the plafond knot. Loop this end around the body of the just-completed cloverleaf knot and tie a two-loop cloverleaf knot into the bottom loop of knot 7. Use the right cord end to repeat the pattern on the right side. Then use the two cord ends, and the looped sections of cord between knots 6 and 7 and knots 6 and 9 to tie another cloverleaf knot. This is just like tying the center knot in a *ju i* knot. Finally, tie a two-loop cloverleaf

27

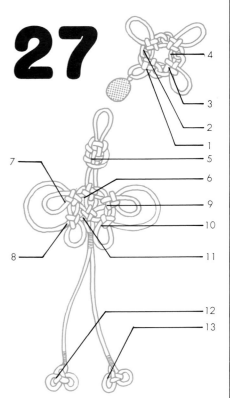

knot onto each of the two cord ends. Turn the ends back on themselves and bind them in place with thread. You might also want to bind the cords together where they emerge from knot 11 for added stability.

28

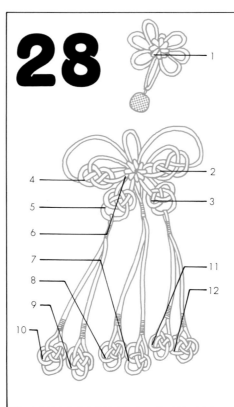

This fastener is quite simple. The button part is a seven-loop round brocade knot, with the button strung onto the lower loop while tying, or sewn on afterwards. Begin the bottom part, a variation of the butterfly knot, with a seven-loop round brocade knot. Tie the first two loops on the right into a double coin knot, and tie another double coin knot into the third loop. Then tie the left side in the same way. After knot 5 is done, completion of the round brocade knot follows. Tie a double coin knot at the end of each of the loose ends, binding the cord to itself with thread just above the knot. Pass new cords through the bottom loops of the butterfly's wings, binding them in place just below the wings, and treating all four cord ends as you treated the other two.

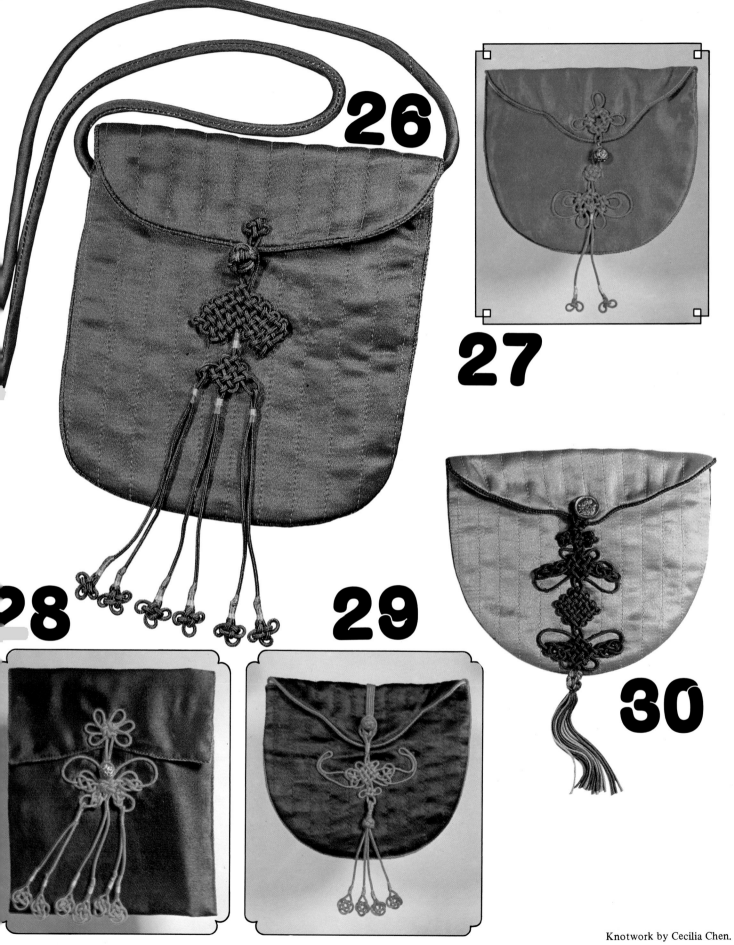

26

27

28

29

30

Knotwork by Cecilia Chen.

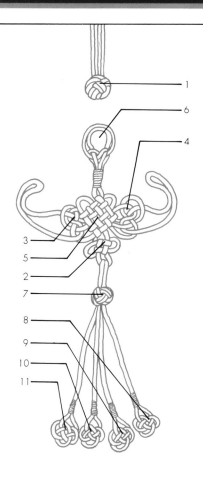

30

This ornament is tied with one cord. Begin at the top with a *ju i* knot. Below this, tie a butterfly knot facing away from the *ju i* knot. Tie a large *pan chang* knot below the butterfly. Add a butterfly knot below the *pan chang*, this time facing the knotting above it. Leave the cord ends hanging as tassels, and add extra ones, if desired.

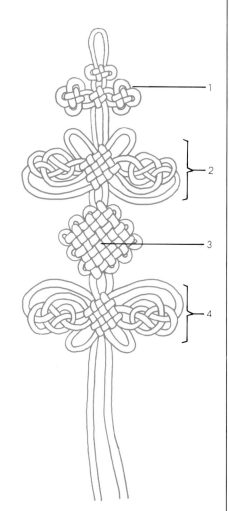

29

This fastener has a very simple top and a more involved bottom portion. The top is a button knot tied with a double cord. Start the bottom with a three-loop cloverleaf knot, knot 2, followed by a *pan chang* knot, working two double coin knots into the outer loops as in the butterfly knot. The wing loops are elongated into the shape of a bat's wings. This is followed by a double coin knot which forms the loop for the button. The free ends are then bent back and tied with a silk thread to the cord between the *pan chang* and double coin knot. Then pass two additional cords through the center loop of the three-loop cloverleaf knot. Tie these two cords as if they were one into a button knot. Let the four loose ends hang free, tying a double coin knot onto each one, and binding each loose end to itself just above the knot.

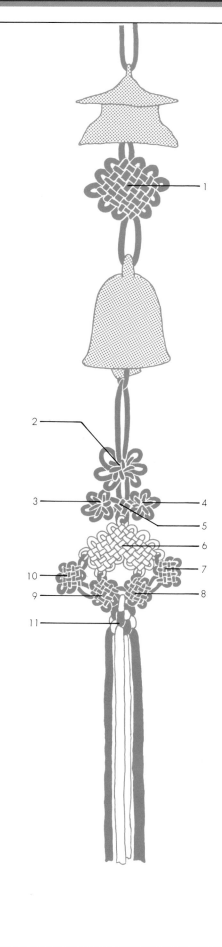

31

Tie the two bells together with a *pan chang* knot, hiding the loose ends in the body of the knot. Use another cord, attaching it to the clapper of the lower bell, to tie a seven-loop round brocade knot. Then use each of the loose ends separately to tie a five-loop round brocade knot, knots 3 and 4. Tie a cloverleaf knot in the center with both of the loose ends and the cord sections between knots 2 and 3 and knots 2 and 4, just like tying the center cloverleaf in a *ju i* knot. Sew the loose ends into the body of the cloverleaf. Pass another cord through its lower loop and use it to tie a stone chime knot, hiding the loose ends in the body of the completed stone chime knot. Then use another cord to tie a horizontal series of four *pan chang* knots, linking the upper corner of each one into the adjacent corner loop of the stone chime knot. Hide the loose ends in the body of the last *pan chang*. Pass two new cords through the center loop between the *pan chang* knots. Use the four loose ends to tie a square column. To tie this square column, cross the cords under each other in one direction, hooking the last one back into the knotwork like you are closing a boxtop. Then repeat the process, crossing them over one another in the opposite direction. This is much like tying a good luck knot, except you are using a single cord instead of loops. Continue tying the column until you reach the desired length; leave the ends dangling.

This decoration, hanging from a bell clapper, is made up of seven cords. Begin with one cord, tying a cloverleaf knot and a *pan chang* knot underneath the clapper. Hide the loose ends in the body of the *pan chang*. Pass another cord through its lower loop and use it to tie a stone chime knot, hiding the loose ends in the body of the completed knot. Pass a new cord through the bottom center loop of the stone chime knot, and tie a series of alternating half hitches. Add a large *pan chang*, more half hitches, a round brocade knot, a small *pan chang*, and more half hitches. End this section with a button knot, hiding the ends of additional tassels in its body. Pass another cord through the outer left corner loop of the stone chime knot. Tie a series of alternating half hitches, a round brocade knot, more half hitches, another round brocade knot, more half hitches, a brocade ball knot, and a button knot, again with tassel ends hidden in the button knot. Use another cord to repeat this pattern off of the outer right corner loop of the stone chime knot. Finally, pass a new cord through the inner left corner loop of the stone chime knot. Tie a series of alternating half hitches, broken in two places with cloverleaf knots, and ending with a button knot, where tassels can be added. Use another cord to tie an identical series off of the inner right corner loop of the stone chime knot.

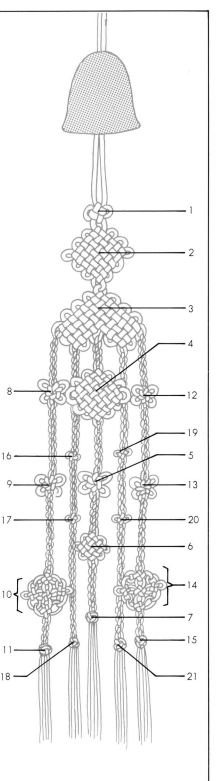

《SEE PAGE 33 FOR A PHOTO OF THE KNOTWORK IN NUMBER 31》

32

33

This ornament is tied with four separate cords. Begin at the top of the *pan chang* configuration, knot 1. Tie two *pan chang* knots, hiding the cord ends in the body of the second one. With another cord, tie two horizontal *pan chang* knots, linking their outer loops into the adjacent outer loops of the *pan chang* knots above and below. Hide the loose ends in the body of the last knot. Then pass another cord through the top loop of the first *pan chang* knot, and tie a double connection knot to hold the cord in place. Moving upwards, tie a *ju i* knot, a cloverleaf knot, and a double connection knot. The loose cords may be tied around any object, in this case a Chinese lantern. Pass another cord through the lower corner loop of the

bottom *pan chang* knot, and use it to tie yet another *pan chang*. Leave extra cord in the two lowest loops of this *pan chang*. Use the left cord end to tie the lower left loop of the *pan chang* into a two-loop cloverleaf knot. When this is finished, the loose end will emerge from the top of the knot, pointing back toward the *pan chang*. Loop this loose end around the body of the two-loop cloverleaf knot, and use it to tie another two-loop cloverleaf knot into the section of cord connecting the *pan chang* and the first two-loop cloverleaf knot. Then use the right cord end to repeat the process on the right side. When this is done, bring the two loose ends together and use them to tie a standard cloverleaf knot in the center, linking its side loops with the adjacent loops of the two-loop cloverleaf knots above it. Finish with a double connection knot, adding tassels in the body of the knot, if desired. The bead is sewn on after the knots are completed.

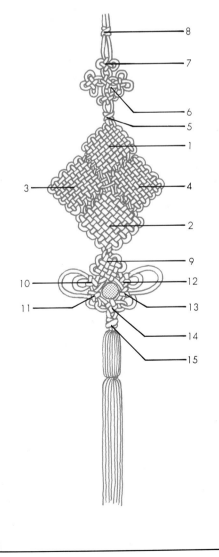

This large wall hanging is tied around a rattan ring. To begin with, enclose the ring with a continuous circle of lock stitches. Tie off the stitching and hide the cord ends within it. Use a new cord to tie a continuous series of two-loop cloverleaf knots on the inside of the ring. Each of the two-loop cloverleaf knots uses the inner part of a lock stitch for one of its two loops. The free end from a completed two-loop cloverleaf knot passes under the stitching before it is used to start another knot. At the center of both sides of the ring, tie a seven-loop round brocade knot to replace one of the two-loop cloverleaf knots. After the circle of inner knots is done, hide the end of the cord in the stitching. Next, pass another cord through the top center two-loop cloverleaf knot in the ring, use it to tie a longevity knot. Link the longevity knot to the inner ring of the two-loop cloverleaf knots at its every extremity, making sure that the links are spaced evenly. Once the inside of the ring is done, turn to the outer edge. There, tie a continuous series of *ju i* knots all the way around the ring. Link the bottom outermost loops of each *ju i* to the respective loop of the *ju i* next to it. Once the circle of *ju i* knots is done, move to the bottom of the ring. Pass a cord through the bottom

center of the knotting on the outside of the ring. Use this cord to tie a double connection and a butterfly knot. Add tassels to the loose ends, wrapping all the cords together. The top outer loops in the butterfly's wings can be stitched to the adjacent loops in the outer edge of the ring for added stability. Next, turn to the top of the ring. Pass a cord through the top center of the ring, and use it to tie a series of three double connection knots. Leave plenty of cord above the last double connection knot. The remaining knots at the top of the ring are started with two separate single cords. Attach each end to the outer edge of knots on the ring. Tie a horizontal series of four double coin knots onto each of the cords. Bring them together and tie a button knot, followed by a large *pan chang* knot. As you are tying the *pan chang*, add a *ju i* on both the left and right corner loops. Finish the *pan chang* and leave the ends free. Return to the loose cord ends coming from the series of double connection knots at the top center of the ring. Pass these ends through the middle of the button knot, and weave them through the *pan chang* knot to come out at the top. All six of the loose ends can then share the weight of the ring when it is hanging.

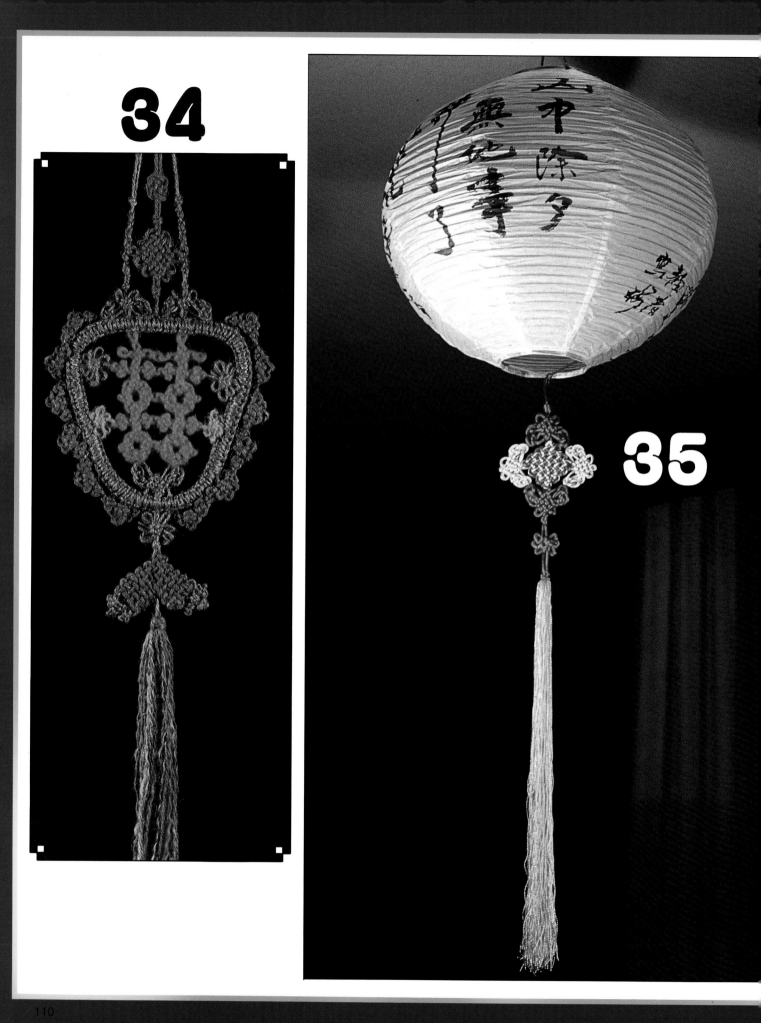

34

35

34

This wall hanging, like creative application 33, uses a rattan ring as the base for the knotting. Begin by tying a continuous series of flat knots around the ring. Then, leaving enough space at the top of the ring to attach the three knotted cords from which the ring will hang, use another cord to tie the series of knots on the outside of the ring. The center of each knot is a round brocade knot with five complete loops. As you tie each of these knots, add a cloverleaf knot to each of the two loops that lie closest to the ring. The loose ends are passed between the flat knots and the ring before they are used to tie another round brocade-cloverleaf combination. Leave enough space at the bottom of the ring for the knotting that will be done below it, and use another cord to repeat the pattern on the other side. Then turn to the inside of the ring. First, pass two cords symmetrically through the series of flat knots at the top of the ring, and use them to tie a double happiness knot, hiding the four loose ends in the body of the knot. Use another cord to tie a six-loop round brocade knot, linking its top loop into the extreme left outer loop of the top bar in the double happiness knot. Attach the loose ends of the round brocade knot to the flat knots on the ring, thus anchoring it and the double happiness knot. Repeat this process with the three other ends of the horizontal bars of the double happiness knot. At the bottom of the double happiness knot, use another cord to tie a butterfly knot. Link the upper loop of each of its wings to the bottom of the double happiness knot. After the butterfly is done, pass the loose ends through the flat knots to come out below the ring. There, tie a round brocade knot with eight loops and a double connection knot. Use another cord to tie a stone chime knot. This knot is attached to the others with the loose ends from the double connection knot hanging off the bottom of the ring. Weave each cord along one of the upper edges of the stone chime knot to emerge at either end of the "L" shape. Tie a *ju i* knot with each cord, and then weave them back into the stone chime knot along each of its lower edges to emerge alongside the loose ends of the stone chime knot itself. Use all four cord ends to tie a double-cord button knot. Leave the loose ends hanging as tassels, or add new cords for a larger tassel, hiding the loose ends in the body of the button knot. Tackle the knotwork at the top of the ring next. Pass three separate cords through the outside of the flat knots, spacing them evenly. The ones on the left and right are tied first. Begin on one side with a butterfly knot facing the ring. Hook the wings through the flat knots on the ring. Tie a double connection knot above the butterfly knot. Continue up with an unbroken series of alternating half hitches. Once you have reached the desired length, finish with another double connection knot. Tie the cord on the other side in the same pattern. Then, with the center cord, tie a double connection knot followed by a large *pan chang* knot. As you tie the *pan chang*, hook the left and right corner loops through the alternating half hitches running alongside them. Finish the *pan chang*, and tie a double connection knot and a plafond knot above it. Bring all six loose ends together above the knotting.

35

This decoration is tied with two cords. Using one cord, tie a double connection knot and a butterfly facing away from it. Then add the second cord and begin a large *pan chang* knot, tying the double cord as if it were one cord. But when you reach the right corner loop, use the second cord only to tie a butterfly knot facing the *pan chang*. Do the same with the left corner loop. Then finish the *pan chang*, and hide the loose ends of the second cord in the body of the knot. Continue with the loose ends from the original cord to tie another butterfly knot facing the *pan chang* knot. Add a double connection knot, a round brocade knot, and a button knot. Tassels can be added, hiding the top ends in the body of the button knot, if desired.

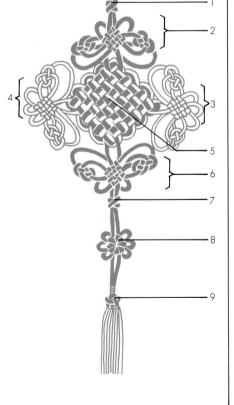

1

2

3

4

5

6

7

8

9

36

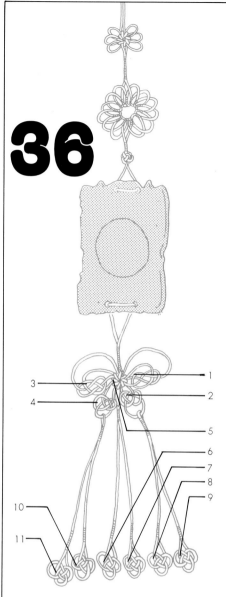

36

3
4
1
2
5
6
7
8
9
10
11

This creation is made up of two independent sets of knots, each tied separately. Begin the bottom set, a variation on the butterfly knot, by stringing the cord through the centerpiece. Start tying a seven-loop round brocade knot. Tie the first two loops on the right into a double coin knot, and tie another double coin knot into the third loop. Then tie the left side in the same way. After knot 4 is done, completion of the round brocade knot follows. Tie a double coin knot at the end of each of the loose ends, binding the cord to itself with thread just above the knot. Pass new cords through the bottom loops of the butterfly's wings, binding them in place just below the wings, and treating all four cord ends as you treated the other two. For the knotting at the top of the

37

piece, run the cord through the centerpiece and tie a button knot directly above it. The next part of the pattern is not a knot at all. Simply lay each cord end in a semicircle of loops and stitch them in place in the center. Bring the semicircles together and sew them to each other at the top. Above this figure, tie a round brocade knot with seven loops. Bind the cords together in strategic locations to hold the knots and the circle of loops in their proper places.

This wall hanging is made up of three large compositions, each tied separately around a rattan ring. After all three rings are done, they are tied together with additional cords.

TOP RING: begin by enclosing the top ring in a continuous series of flat knots. Then use another cord to tie the knots along the outer edge. Following the diagram from the top center down the right side and hooking the cord of each knot under the flat knot series, tie three cloverleaf knots, an unattached cloverleaf knot on top of an attached fifth cloverleaf knot, and two more attached cloverleaf knots. Next, tie an unattached *ju i* knot, which will ride piggyback on an attached eighth cloverleaf knot. Continue with two more attached cloverleaf knots, an unattached cloverleaf knot riding piggyback on an attached twelfth cloverleaf knot, and two more attached cloverleaf knots. Tie the same pattern in reverse order on the left side of the ring, so that you will end up having a total of five attached cloverleaf knots on the top as well as on the bottom. Hide the cord ends in the flat knots. For the middle of the ring, pass a cord through the top of the inside of the flat knot series, and tie a cloverleaf knot. Start a round brocade knot with eight loops below this. As you are tying the round brocade knot, add a cloverleaf knot to each outer loop. Hook the outside loops of the cloverleaf knots into the flat knots on the inside of the ring, and link the side loops of the cloverleaf knots to each other. When the round brocade knot is done, tie another cloverleaf knot beneath it. Link its side loops with the adjacent loops of the other two cloverleaf knots, hook the last loop into the flat knots at the bottom, and hide the cord ends in the body of the knot.

CENTER RING: begin with a series of flat knots around the entire ring. Use another cord to tie the knotwork around the outer edge, hooking each knot that is adjacent to the ring through the flat knots. Begin with a cloverleaf knot at the top center. Start another cloverleaf knot next to it, but when you reach the extreme outer loop, start to tie it into a six-loop round brocade knot. When you reach the extreme outer loop of the round brocade knot, tie it into a cloverleaf knot. Then proceed back to finish the round brocade knot and the cloverleaf knot at its base. Then tie a cloverleaf knot next to this figure, with another cloverleaf knot tied into its extreme outer loop. Next to this, repeat the cloverleaf, round brocade, cloverleaf figure. Follow it with another double cloverleaf combination, and another cloverleaf, round brocade, cloverleaf figure. Finish this side with a single cloverleaf at the bottom center of the ring, and continue up the other side, tying a mirror image of the same knotting pattern. Hide the loose ends of the cord in the flat knots at the top. The middle of this ring is simply a round brocade knot with ten loops. It is tied separately and sewn into the inner edge of the ring.

BOTTOM RING: again start by encasing the ring in a continuous series of flat knots. The outer edge of the ring is tied exactly like that of the top ring, except that here there are three less cloverleaf knots between the stacked cloverleaf knots at the top center of the ring. The number of knots around the edge of the ring varies according to the size of the ring and the thickness of the cord. The number of cloverleaf knots you'll need to complete your design may therefore be more or less than the number indicated for this particular knotwork. To begin the middle of the ring, pass a cord through the top center flat knot and tie a six-loop round brocade knot. Use each single cord to tie another six-loop round brocade knot, hooking each one into the flat knots on its respective side, and linking them with the first round brocade knot. Then use both loose ends and the two sections of cord connecting the three round brocade knots to tie a cloverleaf knot, just like tying the center cloverleaf in a *ju i* knot. Use both ends to tie a final six-loop round brocade knot, linking it to the two adjacent ones. Hook the bottom loop into the flat knots at the bottom; hide the loose ends in the knot.

CONNECTING THE RINGS: to connect the center ring to the top ring, pass a new cord through the center top loop of the center ring. Tie a button knot and a *pan chang* knot, hooking the last two loops of the *pan chang* into the bottom of the top ring, and hiding the loose ends in the body of the knot. A mirror image of this connects the center ring to the bottom ring. Finally, tie a butterfly knot at the top of the top ring, making it face the ring, and linking the butterfly's head and wings to the loops in the outer circle of knotting. Then tie another butterfly knot at the bottom of the bottom ring, again facing the ring, but linking only the head to the knotting on the ring. Stitch the wings in place and tie a button knot below the butterfly. Add extra tassels if desired, hiding their ends within the button knot.

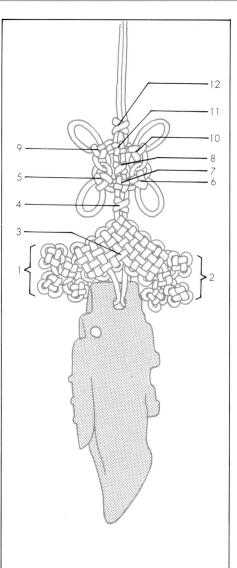

38

This piece of knotwork is done with one cord. Start with a stone chime knot, adding a *ju i* knot to each of the center loops in the short ends. Then pass the free ends through the pendant, and weave them back up through the body of the stone chime knot to come out at the top. Tie a double connection knot. Then tie a two-loop cloverleaf knot with the left cord end and another one with the right cord end. Use both cord ends and the two sections of cord connecting the two-loop cloverleaf knots with the double connection knot to tie a standard cloverleaf knot. Then tie a double connection knot. Repeat the process above, ending with a final double connection knot.

39

This pendant is actually a double diamond knot tied with two separate cords. Begin with a double connection knot at the top, and tie a stone chime knot below it. Hide the loose ends in the body of the stone chime. Use another cord to tie a large *pan chang* below it, hooking the upper loops into the bottom loops of the stone chime knot. When it is completed, tie a button knot below it. String the pendant onto the loose ends before hiding them back into the body of the knot.

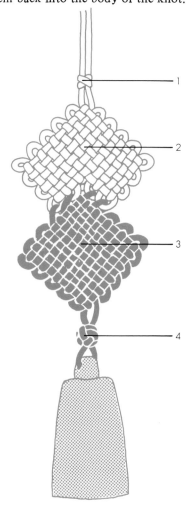

40

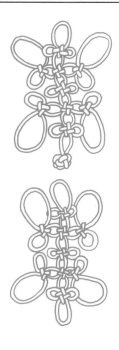

These are some examples of knotted clothes fasteners, each tied with adaptations of the basic and compound knots. Shown clockwise from upper left are: a pair of longevity knots that can be buttoned, a double happiness fastener, a button made of a *pan chang* knot with *ju i* knots tied into three of its corners that fastens into a loop with the same combination attached to it, a small *pan chang* button with a large *pan chang* loop, and a round brocade knot which buttons into a butterfly. These fasteners are easy to tie if you remember a simple rule. Start the button side from the button knot and work out; start the loop side from the loop and work out.

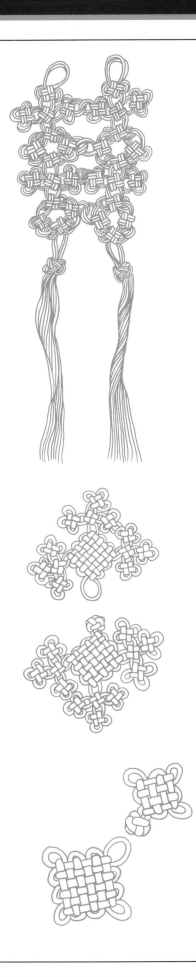

41

This necklace is made in two separate sections. Begin with the chain of knots that goes around the neck. Use a double cord to tie a button knot, hiding one pair of loose ends in the body of the knot. Use the other pair of loose ends, tying them as if they were one cord, to tie a series of double coin knots. When you reach the desired length, make a loop large enough to accommodate the button knot, and bind the cord ends to themselves. Pass a thin wire around the backs of the double coin knots, stitching it to each of them. The pendant is tied from the bottom up, and attached after it is completed. Begin with a single cord, using it to tie a *ju i* knot. Then add a second cord to the loose ends and begin a large *pan chang* knot, tying the two cords as if they were one. On each

side of the *pan chang*, use the second cord to tie a double coin knot out of the two loops in the center of each side. Pull the loops of the first cord tight against the body of the *pan chang*. At each corner loop, use the first cord to tie a *ju i* knot, pulling the loop of the second cord tight against the body. These outer knots are tied in the sequence numbered in the diagram. When they are finished, completion of the *pan chang* follows. Hide the loose ends of the second cord in the body of the *pan chang*, and use the loose ends of the first cord to tie a final *ju i* knot. Add a double connection knot, pass the cord ends through the bottom center loop of the double coin knot chain of the necklace, loop them back, and hide them in the body of the double connection knot.

THE AUTHOR

Born in Loching, Chekiang, in 1940, Lydia Chen received her Bachelor of Science degree in agricultural chemistry from National Chung Hsing University in 1963. Her interest in traditional knotting was born when her father-in-law, Chuang Shang-yen, the Deputy Curator of the National Palace Museum, encouraged her to learn how to tie a few simple knots from an elderly Museum custodian. From this modest beginning, she went on to master the art, first learning the 13 knots in ECHO Magazine, and later figuring out how knots ornamenting the antiques she hunted down were tied. She taught knotting at the Shih Chien College of Home Economics from the fall of 1978 through the spring of 1980, and she has had seven exhibitions of her own knotwork — three in Taipei and one in New York, Korea, and Singapore respectively. She is today the nation's foremost authority on traditional Chinese decorative knotting.

THE ASSOCIATE EDITOR

Yao Meng-chia, born in Taipei, Taiwan, in 1946, received his Bachelor of Arts degree in painting from the National Academy of Arts in 1968. He has been with ECHO since its birth in 1971, and is a key part of the staff. He was responsible for much of the material in the ECHO Magazine articles on Chinese knotting, which included detailed explanations and step-by-step diagrams for the tying of 13 simple knots. With that experience under his belt, he undertook the supervision of all the illustration work in *Chinese Knotting*, making sure that the step-by-step diagrams that accompany each knot were done correctly and presented in the most lucid manner possible.